ISLAMIC
TILES

ISLAMIC TILES

—Venetia Porter—

Interlink Books
An imprint of Interlink Publishing Group, Inc.
NEW YORK

First American edition published in 1995 by

INTERLINK BOOKS
An imprint of Interlink Publishing Group, Inc.
99 Seventh Avenue
Brooklyn, New York 11215

Library of Congress Cataloging-in-Publication Data available

ISBN 1–56656–191–4

FRONT COVER Detail of a rectangular stone-paste tile, underglaze-painted, from
a border panel. Iznik, second half of 16th century. 20×28.8 cm (OA G.1983.85
Godman Bequest).

FRONTISPIECE Cenotaph of the Imam Jalal al-Din ʿAli. Kashan, lustre tiles
(fig. 48), first half of 14th century. HT: 131 cm.

Printed and bound in Italy

10 9 8 7 6 5 4 3 2 1

Contents

PREFACE

T he subject of Islamic tiles is a vast one. I have therefore attempted to write a book that could both act as a guide to the British Museum collection and be useful as a general introduction. The collection of tiles in the British Museum is rich and varied, and strong in several areas, particularly medieval Iran and the Ottoman empire. There are rare types and dated pieces, as well as fragments from archaeological contexts, all of which are of great value to the student of the subject. Its strength is largely a result of donations by and purchase from discerning collectors, those whose imagination was fired by a love of Orientalia, such as John Henderson or Sir Augustus Wollaston Franks, the latter a Keeper in the Museum and a collector in his own right; and travellers such as Percy Sykes, the well-known historian of Persia who collected rare fragments on the ground. The largest collection, a gift from the heirs of F. DuCane Godman, came to the Museum in 1983.

One of the fascinating aspects of working on tiles is trying to piece together tile panels and friezes that were broken up when they were sold on the market in the nineteenth century and subsequently dispersed throughout the world. I recently came across a tile fragment from a rare group produced for an early four-teenth-century shrine at Natanz in Iran, of which we have examples in the collection, in the garden of a house at Kew in London.

In this book the discussion is centred on tiles from the Islamic heartlands. Apart from the ninth-century tiles in Qairouan, those of North Africa and Spain have been excluded as a subject too large to be dealt with here, and there is only a short discussion on

Indian tiles. Although the majority of the illustrations are of tiles in the British Museum, a small number from other collections have been included to complete the story, with a few photographs of tiles in situ added to provide context. Nothing could ever surpass the work of Arthur Lane, a Keeper of Ceramics in the Victoria and Albert Museum, whose books on Islamic pottery and tiles remain inspired and standard works. This contribution attempts, within the limits of space, to bring the subject up to date by reflecting recent research. The works listed under Further Reading (page 124) have been grouped by chapter. Much new material is generally found in articles in journals but only the most accessible of these have been included here.

The term Islamic as used here refers to all objects produced (whether for religious or secular use) in those lands where the dominant religion and its associated political system was Islam, as revealed to the Prophet Muhammad in Mecca in the early seventh century AD. Dates are given according to the Christian rather than the Islamic calendar unless the object under discussion is dated, and transliteration of Arabic words has been simplified throughout.

It only remains for me to thank a number of friends and colleagues, both in the British Museum and elsewhere, who kindly read through the text, made many invaluable suggestions and helped in a variety of other ways (any mistakes are mine): James Allan, Alice Brinton, Andrew Burnett, Sheila Canby, John Carswell, Vesta Curtis, Abdullah Guchani, Jessica Harrison-Hall, Regina Krahl, Judith Lerner, Bernard O'Kane, Julian Raby, Jessica Rawson, Julian Reade, Michael Rogers, St John Simpson, Rachel Ward, Oliver Watson and Mark Zebrowski. For assistance with non-British Museum photographs I am most grateful to Michael Meinecke and Almut von Gladis, Edmund de Unger, Jeanne Moulierac, Qasem Toueir, Stefano Carboni and Margaret Oliphant. For endlessly ferrying the British Museum tiles to the photographers, my thanks go to all the museum assistants in the Department of Oriental Antiquities, in particular Michelle Morgan. For the beautiful photographs I am indebted to David Gowers, John Williams and Lisa Bliss, for the marvellous drawings to Ann Searight and Eva Wilson and for the design of the book to Grahame Dudley. Without Celia Clear, who originally inspired me, and my editor Nina Shandloff, whose patience, kindness and tact apparently know no bounds, this book would not have happened at all. Finally, I affectionately dedicate this book to Charles and Emily, who have put up with Islamic tiles for so long.

— 1 —

CRAFTSMEN AND TECHNIQUES

Tilework was a favourite means of decorating architecture throughout the Islamic lands. Together with mural painting and stucco, tiles brought colour and lavish designs to mosques and shrines, palaces and private houses. Employed in different ways depending on the building material of the region and whether for internal or exterior use, tiles seem to have grown naturally as an adjunct to brick architecture. From tiny exterior elements of colour in brick façades, they end up clothing entire buildings in the fourteenth to fifteenth-century monuments of Timurid Central Asia. In the western Islamic lands, with mainly stone architecture, tilework created a very different but equally dramatic effect through brilliant polychrome tiles against grey stone walls in the buildings of sixteenth and seventeenth-century Turkey.

The history of Islamic tilework is inextricably linked to the production of ceramic vessels and tableware. This is particularly evident in the ceramics of the Seljuqs, Mamluks and Ottomans, whose designs and techniques for vessels often mirror those used for tiles, and the same potters were clearly working on both. Only in the Timurid and Safavid periods are the production techniques so divergent that they were evidently the result of quite distinct industries with separate workshops.

THE TILEMAKERS

As in so much Islamic art, it is only at intermittent periods that tilemakers signed their work. The great exceptions are the well-documented potting families of Kashan in central Iran such as the Abu Tahir, who are known to have been active between the twelfth and fourteenth centuries from numerous signed works, particularly tiles, in mosques and shrines throughout Iran. Another example is the nineteenth-century Iranian potter ʿAli Muhammad Isfahani, from whom Sir Robert Murdoch Smith commissioned work including a treatise on ceramic production.

Other groups of tiles provide us with names but nothing further is known about the craftsmen. From the late fourteenth to the sixteenth century numerous tiles are signed by craftsmen connected with the city of Tabriz, in north-west Iran, such as 'the masters of Tabriz' in Bursa in Turkey, among whom was 'Muhammad the Mad'; Muhammad b. Yusuf al-Tabrizi, at the late fourteenth-century Aq Sarai at Shahr-i Sabz in Central Asia; and Ghaibi al-Tawrizi, on Mamluk tiles from Damascus. Where signatures are found they are often preceded by the word ʿamal (the work of). It must often have been the case that those who made the tiles were not the same as those who decorated them. However, on an important tile in the Cairo Museum dated AH 600/AD 1203–4 and made by the Kashan potter Abu Zaid, the inscription uses the verbs sanaʾa, (to make) and ʿamala (perhaps in this context to decorate), which seems to suggest that he performed both functions. When dates are inscribed on tiles these are either given in numerals or spelled out in letters. On the late thirteenth-century star tiles from the palace of Takht-i Sulayman a combination of the two was used.

It is difficult to estimate the size of the ceramic workshops or to assess how they were organised. However, a study of a traditional workshop in the Maybod district of Yazd in central Iran, undertaken in the mid 1960s, revealed a system that may closely resemble that of the medieval period. A strict hierarchy was in operation, headed by the ustad or master craftsman, who guarded his secrets jealously and had a number of apprentices, mostly members of his own family, working under him. The jobs in the Maybod workshop were clearly delineated, as were the activities undertaken at different times of the year: in the spring and summer the potters worked outside on the roof applying slips, glazes and decoration, while in the winter they worked inside. The warm workshop also fulfilled a social function as the place where the men from the village would gather together in the afternoons and evenings.

9

Once they had finished their training, many of the apprentices went off to start their own potteries in other locations, while others remained in the workshop, carrying on the tradition within the family. References to potters moving from southern Iraq to Samarra in central Iraq in the ninth century and the finds of kilns at Takht-i Sulayman clearly demonstrate that potters in the medieval period moved around to work on special commissions. Keeping the industry within the family ensured that skills remained alive and explains, in part, the inherent conservatism of style, with techniques and designs often appearing with little variation for over a century or longer.

The study of the Maybod workshops also provides some insight into the changing social and economic status of potters. In the early part of this century, potters who worked on the still sought-after stone-paste vessels (using a man-made quartz-based material, described below) rather than the utilitarian earthenware were relatively wealthy and enjoyed some social distinction. This had undoubtedly been the case for the more prominent Kashan lustre potters in the thirteenth century. As with all crafts, however, once patronage and demand waned the potters inevitably suffered unless they were lucky enough to be able to use their skills elsewhere. In Morocco, for instance, where locally made household pottery has been largely superseded by imported china, potters have been able to find work in workshops producing *zillij* (tile mosaic), for which demand still exists.

KILNS AND MOULDS

1,2 The kilns used in the Islamic world were updraught kilns, round or oval structures consisting of two chambers. The lower chamber consisted of the firebox, separated from the upper firing chamber by a perforated floor. The heat passed into the cavity above the firebox through the holes in the floor, circulated within this upper chamber in which the pottery was contained, and came out through the holes in the domed roof. Abu'l Qasim, historian of the Mongol court and member of the Abu Tahir family of potters, described the kilns in a manuscript dated AD 1301 as follows:

This is like a high tower and inside has row upon row of earthenware pegs . . . fitted into holes in the wall. The vessels are placed on them and fired for twelve hours with a hot even fire, with this stipulation that no wood be put on until the smoking has stopped, so that the smoke does not ruin or blacken the pots. In Kashan they burn soft wood (like hyssop and walnut) and in Baghdad, Tabriz and other places the wood of a willow

1 OPPOSITE Kiln excavated in Benaket east of Merv, c.10th–11th century. The row of holes would have held the pegs on which the pottery sat.

lid of kiln

long ceramic pegs on
which the objects sat

2m

arrows show heat
passing from firebox
into cavity

ground level

1m

firebox

1.8m

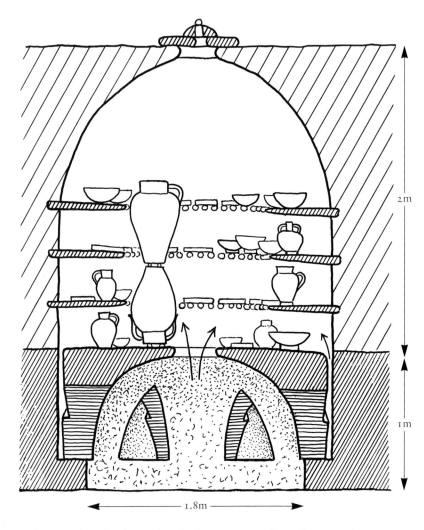

2 Reconstruction of a
kiln excavated at the
13th-century palace of
Takht-i Sulayman.

stripped of its bark so that it does not smoke. The vessels are
removed from the kiln after a week.

Kilns with rows of earthenware pegs between 60 and 70 cm long
have been unearthed at a number of sites, including Siraf on the
Persian Gulf, in Central Asia and the Il-Khanid palace of Takht-i-
Sulayman, and were still used in traditional potteries earlier this
century. Vessels and tiles would have been placed on these pegs,
sometimes in earthenware cases called saggars, to protect them
from the direct heat of the fire (Abu'l Qasim mentions saggars
used in Iran). The loading of the kiln was a skilled task as the
objects could be spoiled if they were unevenly placed, particularly
for the biscuit (first) firing, or if the draught somehow became
blocked. Alan Caiger-Smith has pointed out that kilns in pre-
modern times were not intended to be long lasting and the

kilns were usually rebuilt after only one or just a few firings.

Tiles would generally have been made in moulds, which were particularly practical for repeat patterns. Oliver Watson has suggested that the moulds for small Kashan star tiles are likely to have been used repeatedly whereas the process for manufacturing the large frieze tiles was more complicated and seems to have involved a basic mould containing designs for the upper and lower sections only. The inscriptions or moulded designs of the central section would have been applied separately. The technique of making tiles in moulds used by traditional potters in Iran is described by Hans Wulff (writing in the 1960s) as follows:

The tilemaker usually works in the open air. His assistant prepares suitably sized clay lumps. The master has a wooden mould in front of him and throws the clay lump into it with verve, beats it with his bare hands to force it into the remote corners of the mould, folds the surplus up, and cuts it away with a wire. Then he empties the mould with a swift movement. The assistant takes the tiles into the shade for the first stage of drying and when they have sufficient strength he places them in a well-ventilated drying room, face down on the flat floor, for the slow and final drying.

THE MATERIALS: CLAY AND STONE-PASTE

Until about the twelfth century AD, the material used to make both luxury vessels and tiles was clay. Its quality depended on what was available and how it was treated – for example, the ʿAbbasid clay used for tiles and vessels is very pure and was evidently finely sifted. Clay continued to be used for utilitarian objects such as water storage jars (as it still is today in the Middle East) and occasionally for more sophisticated pottery. However, by the twelfth century, a man-made material known as stone-paste or fritware had been developed and was being used in Egypt, Syria and Iran.

The impetus for the production of stone-paste was the desire to imitate the fineness and translucency of imported Chinese porcelain of the Song dynasty (AD 960–1279). It was made, according to a recipe given by Abu'l Qasim, from ten parts ground quartz mixed with one part glaze frit and one part fine white clay. The ground quartz was obtained from pebbles collected from dry river beds or from sand. The glaze frit, which served to hold the ground quartz together, was made from a combination of pounded quartz and calcinated soda plant, heated until it melted into clear glass. The third important element was a pure white clay which often had to be brought from far afield. (The Maybod potters brought it from a site about 200 km away.)

The composition of stone-paste is very similar to that of the material often called faience, employed by the potters of ancient Egypt and in pre-Islamic Iran for making beads and during the Achaemenid period (539–330 BC) for glazed bricks. Why its use disappeared until about the twelfth century AD is a mystery. Once rediscovered, the material proved very popular and has been used almost continuously in some parts of the Islamic world up to the present day. A recipe given by the nineteenth-century Persian potter ʿAli Muhammad Isfahani describes virtually the same components as does Abuʾl Qasim. Although it was a difficult material to throw, as recently demonstrated by experiments carried out at the school of art in Farnham, Surrey, the combined strength and malleability of the material enabled a greater fineness and versatility of shape as well as new possibilities for decoration, especially with the adoption of an alkaline-based glaze which provided greater stability for the coloured pigments painted under the glaze.

GLAZES

A glaze distinguishes luxury from utilitarian pottery. The glassy surface has two functions, decorative and functional. An unglazed vessel will allow its liquid contents to seep out while a glaze renders it impermeable. Glazed tiles not only enriched the surface of the architecture they decorated, but also provided protection from the elements for the walls of the building.

In the early Islamic period a lead glaze – that is, a glaze fluxed with lead oxide – was the principal glaze used. (A flux is the substance which lowers the melting or fusion point of a glaze.) This had the peculiar property of causing the colours painted under it to run, a fault turned to good effect in vessels of the ʿAbbasid period known as 'splashed wares'. At different times Islamic potters employed a variety of techniques to counter the running effect. While the tenth-century Nishapur potters resorted to mixing their pigments with slip (liquid clay), the ʿAbbasid potters came up with a different solution. They developed a thick opaque white glaze which served to hide the clay ground and over which they painted their designs. This is usually called a tin glaze, a term which can be misleading. Although tin (mined in Malaysia, Burma and Cornwall and exported to the Middle East) was indeed often used to opacify the glaze, and Abuʾl Qasim certainly mentions that the Kashan potters used tin oxide mixed with lead oxide for this purpose, it now appears that methods and materials other than tin were sometimes used: the mineral antimony appears in analyses of early Islamic pottery from Susa in Iran, while analyses of sherds from Siraf show that opacification was achieved by firing alkaline glazes at low temperatures so as to leave numerous unvitrified particles in suspension.

In the twelfth century an alkaline glaze – a glaze fluxed with soda or potash – was developed in conjunction with the stone-paste body. As with the lead glaze, it could either be used in a transparent colourless form or pigments could be added to it. Pigments painted under it, if care was taken, generally did not run. It could be rendered white by the addition of an opacifying agent as with the ground of Kashan tiles. Opaque turquoise, a popular colour for both vessels and tiles, was produced through a combination of the alkaline glaze, tin and copper.

TECHNIQUES OF DECORATION

The principal techniques used in the decoration of Islamic tile-work are lustre, underglaze painting and overglaze painting (*minai* and *lajvardina*), tile mosaic and *cuerda seca*, some for internal use only, such as lustre and *minai*, the others employed inside and out.

Lustre

In the context of ceramics, the word 'lustre' describes a metallic sheen giving off multi-coloured reflections. The technique, first used in Egypt in the eighth century to decorate glass, was probably adopted in Basra in Iraq and was there transferred to pottery. Lustre tiles were first made in about the ninth century and are found at Samarra in Iraq and at the Great Mosque at Qairouan in Tunisia. The most brilliant period of lustre tile production was between the twelfth and fourteenth centuries at the potteries of Kashan.

3

3 Detail of 13th-century stone-paste Kashan star lustre tile.

4 Back of eight-pointed Kashan star tile, dated AH 660/ AD 1261–2, showing a lustre shadow transferred from another tile during firing. DIAM: 31 cm.

The production of lustre is both a mysterious and complicated process. It is achieved by applying a mixture of silver and copper oxides to the cold surface of a glazed vessel or tile. This is then fired again in a reduction kiln (in which the air supply is restricted, producing carbon monoxide), which extracts oxygen from the oxides and reduces them to a pure metallic state in which they become fixed to the surface. Once out of the kiln, the objects are lightly rubbed to remove any earthy deposit and, as evocatively described by Abu'l Qasim, 'that which has been evenly fired reflects like red gold and shines like the light of the sun'. A curious feature seen on the backs of a number of thirteenth-century lustre tiles is the imprint of a lustre design, which shows that the **4** tiles were packed very closely during the second firing.

The construction of the kiln was a crucial factor, as were the positions of the objects inside the kiln and the type and amount of fuel used. The Italian potter Piccolpasso, writing in 1558, says:

Many make [the lustre kilns] on the floors of houses which are locked and under close guard for they look to the manner of making the kiln as an important secret and say that in this consists the whole art . . . the art is treacherous for oft times of one hundred pieces of ware tried in the fire, scarce six are good.

It is certain therefore that lustre was not a technique that could be learned simply from seeing the objects; craftsmen were needed to teach it. In addition, the continuity of designs on lustre pottery between the ninth and fourteenth centuries indicates that the lustre potters travelled between centres of patronage, taking the technique with them.

Underglaze and overglaze painting

5 The most successful attempts at underglaze painting were achieved after the discovery of the frit body in the twelfth century. The colours were painted either directly on the body or on a thin quartzy surface and then glazed with a transparent colourless or copper blue alkaline glaze. At Kashan the technique was more generally used on pots, although it is found on some relief-moulded tiles, and turquoise and cobalt splashes are often combined with lustre on tiles. The technique did not come into its own until the fifteenth century in Egypt and Syria. Its most spectacular use, however, was on the Ottoman pottery and tilework of Iznik in Turkey, and it was also used by the Qajar potters of Iran during the nineteenth and twentieth centuries.

At Kashan the potters also developed the technique of painting in coloured pigments over as well as under the glaze, a technique known as minai (from the Arabic mina, meaning glaze) or haft rang (seven, i.e. many, colours). This was a technique commonly used on late twelfth-century vessels, but more rarely on tiles. From the second half of the thirteenth century and continuing well into the fourteenth, an associated technique called lajvardina (from the Persian for lapis lazuli or cobalt) was also adopted. In this technique various colours including white, red and angular shapes of gold leaf were applied over a cobalt blue or turquoise ground. Abu'l Qasim describes applying gold on lajvardina as follows:

If they want to gild transparent or opaque pieces they hammer a mithqal of red gold in 24 sheets putting paper covered with plaster between them. They cut carefully with scissors and stick them with a pen on to vessels with dissolved glue and smooth them with cotton.

Tile mosaic and cuerda seca

Tile mosaic, cut tilework and mosaic faience are the various terms used to describe a technique which was first adopted in Anatolia in the early thirteenth century and appeared in Iran and Central Asia a century later. It was described by Arthur Lane:

5 Hexagonal stone-paste tile, painted in black under a green glaze, with traces of overglaze gold. Second half of 15th century. It is not yet known for certain where tiles from this group were made. There are numerous examples dispersed in a number of collections. A parallel may be drawn with another similar group in situ in the tomb chamber of the Masjid-i Shah at Mashhad, dated 1451. DIAM: 15.5 cm.

Slabs of glazed tile were cut after firing into shapes that interlocked and formed a continuous surface of pattern in contrasted colours . . . The individual pieces . . . were fitted together face downwards on a cartoon of the design; plaster poured over the back and between the bevels, and strengthened by inset canes running crossways bound into panels which when dry could be lifted and placed in position against the wall.

At Timur's late thirteenth-century palace Aq Sarai at Shahr-i Sabz 7 in Central Asia, the imprint of the pieces of tile mosaic which have fallen out of the clay panels can be clearly seen. Recent research in Morocco has shown that tile mosaic (there known as *zillij*) had to be cut after firing because, if cut before, the pieces tended to shrink. Indeed, tilemakers had to calculate the shrinkage factor for all tiles in assessing the size and number needed for covering any given surface.

A technique developed side by side with tile mosaic during the latter part of the fourteenth century in Central Asia was *cuerda* 6 *seca*, literally meaning in Spanish 'dry cord'. Complete tiles were painted with coloured pigments which were separated from each

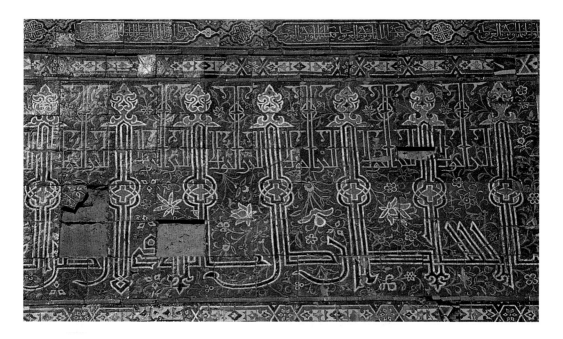

6 ABOVE Detail of *cuerda seca* inscriptional tiles painted with gold, in situ at the Timurid Aq Sarai palace at Shahr-i Sabz (1379–96).

7 BELOW Detail of tile mosaic in situ at the Aq Sarai palace at Shahr-i Sabz. The imprint of tiles which have fallen out of the clay base can be seen at the top of the photograph.

8 17th-century Safavid tile with blue and turquoise glazes laid over a white glaze ground. The inscription in square Kufic script is the Qur'anic phrase 'Allah there is no God but He'.

other to prevent them from running by an oily substance mixed with manganese, which left a dark outline after firing. On some tiles gold leaf and red, as on *lajvardina* ware, were also applied. The technique was widely used during the Timurid and Safavid periods to produce tiles for covering large surfaces. Persian potters from Tabriz in the fifteenth century were responsible for transmitting the *cuerda seca* technique to Turkey.

In the following chapters we shall see how these techniques were developed, some such as *minai* appearing briefly and disappearing, others like lustre and 'tin glaze' continuing throughout the Islamic period and ultimately influencing European pottery.

—2—

'LIKE THE LIGHT OF THE SUN'

LUSTRE TILES

9TH–11TH CENTURIES

The story of Islamic tilework begins in the ninth century, although in the pre-Islamic period tilework had a long tradition both in Egypt and the ancient Near East. In Egypt glazed tiles were used from as early as the Third Dynasty (c.2780–2680 BC). Interesting examples glazed in greenish-blue and designed to imitate reed matting were found at the Step Pyramid of Zoser at Saqqara, while glazed and moulded tiles with natural-istic plant and animal forms come from the New Kingdom site of Amarna (1372–1350 BC). In Assyria glazed bricks were often used in both palaces and temples to form magnificent panoramic friezes, and in an inscription attributable to Tiglath-pileser (1114–1076 BC) he refers to his palace embellished with brightly coloured glazed bricks. Assyrian glazed bricks were used in a vari-ety of ways: glazed either on the square side like a tile, on one edge only, or moulded and glazed. There are fine examples of ninth-century BC tiles from Ashur depicting charioteers, and, from Nimrud, of the king and his attendants. Evocative descriptions of glazed brick decoration at Babylon are recorded by the classical authors. Ctesias, for instance, writing in the fourth century BC, says, 'on both the towers and walls are animals of every kind in-geniously executed by the use of colours . . . the whole had been made to represent a hunt, complete in every detail of all sorts of wild animals and their size more than four cubits'. The descrip-

9

9 Earthenware glazed tile from Nimrud, probably from the reign of Ashurnasirpal II (883–859 BC), painted in yellow and black, depicting the Assyrian king drinking with his attendants. HT: 30 cm.

tions are borne out by excavation and reconstruction, although the scenes that Ctesias was probably referring to were not actually hunting scenes but a variety of different animals, some of them mythical. Particularly striking is the brilliant blue glaze and the animals in high relief on the Ishtar Gate (c.600 BC), now in Berlin. Under the Achaemenids (539–330 BC) glazed elements were also used in architecture.

Whereas Assyrian and Babylonian glazed bricks were made of clay, the Achaemenid examples were made from a coarse quartz body akin to the stone-paste or fritware of twelfth-century AD Kashan. The coloured glazes were contained within raised black lines made from iron oxide (the same principle was used in the *cuerda seca* tiles of Timurid Central Asia, except that the latter used manganese rather than iron oxide). Fine examples of Achaemenid glazing are known from Persepolis and from the fifth to fourth-century Achaemenid palace at Susa, from which a panel depicting an archer is displayed in the British Museum. Although the use of glazed bricks continued intermittently in the Seleucid period (c.330–150 BC) it gradually died out, so that by the beginning of the Islamic period although vessels were glazed, glazed bricks were no longer an architectural feature.

In the Mediterranean lands under Roman and Byzantine domination, painting and mosaic rather than tilework were the principal forms of architectural decoration. The early Islamic

buildings of Syria and Palestine, the Umayyad mosque of Damascus (AD 706) and the Dome of the Rock in Jerusalem (AD 692) carry
on this tradition and are decorated with elaborate mosaics,
whereas the early palaces were richly painted with frescoes. It may
be a deliberate evocation of the pre-Islamic past or, since there is
no stylistic connection, more likely sheer coincidence that the first
Islamic tiles appeared in ninth-century Iraq, in a region where the
Assyrians and Achaemenids had used glazed bricks in their architecture a millennium before.

Islamic history begins with the *Hijra* (flight) of the Prophet
Muhammad from Mecca, where he was born, to Medina where he
set up his community founded on the principles revealed to him
by Allah in the Muslim holy book, the Qur'an. Under the Prophet
and his four immediate successors, the 'rightly guided caliphs'
(AD 632–61), the young state rapidly expanded out of Arabia,
conquering territories previously held by the Byzantines in the
west and the Sasanians in the east. By AD 661, the early Islamic
state had become a great Islamic empire with the first of the major
dynasties, the Umayyads, established in Syria with their capital at
Damascus.

After the fall of the Umayyad dynasty in AD 750, the focus of
the Islamic empire shifted from Syria to Iraq where their successors, the ʿAbbasids, ruled from Baghdad. Under the early ʿAbbasid
caliphs, Baghdad became not only the capital of a vast empire that
stretched from North Africa to India, but also a centre of culture
and learning where literature, science and the arts flourished.

Under the ʿAbbasids, in marked contrast to the undistinguished
pottery of a mostly utilitarian kind made during the Umayyad
period, an extraordinarily sophisticated group of ceramic wares
was produced. Tilework formed only a very small part of the production. The main emphasis was on the manufacture of vessels,
the range and quality of which are outstanding. Tableware richly
painted in 'splashes' of green and brown, in delicate cobalt blue
or in lustre was made in large quantities and exported widely –
examples have been found as far away as Brahminabad in Sindh,
in Sri Lanka and in Thailand. However, tilework has only been
found at two sites so far, at the Jawsaq al-Khaqani palace at
Samarra in Iraq and at the Great Mosque at Qairouan in Tunisia.

The development of the ceramics industry during the early
ʿAbbasid period cannot be understood without reference to
Chinese porcelain. Tang wares were the first in a series of waves
of Chinese ceramics imported into the Near East that would exert
a profound influence on Islamic potters both technically and stylistically. The potters were inspired by the whiteness and purity of

the imported white wares, which have been found at numerous sites all over the Middle East. However, unable to reproduce porcelain itself, their earliest products were cosmetic imitations of porcelain in earthenware: finely potted, with a characteristically yellow-buff dense clay body that was to be a hallmark of all ʿAbbasid pottery, and covered with a milky white 'tin glaze'.

Of most concern to us here is lustre, which, apart from the use of plain green or yellow glazes, was the main technique used on tiles of the ʿAbbasid period. ʿAbbasid lustre ware – both vessels and tiles – falls into two main stylistic categories. The earliest group, decorated in polychrome lustre, have designs that contain echoes of Sasanian or classical motifs. The links with the glass industry, where lustre was first used, are evident, particularly the 'peacock eye' motif, a characteristic of ʿAbbasid lustre derived from the designs on Roman *millefiori* glass. The later group are monochrome lustre, with some of the vessels decorated with figures that seem to be drawn from Central Asian Buddhist art.

THE TILES OF SAMARRA

Samarra, one of the most important archaeological sites in the Islamic world, was first surveyed in 1907. Shortly before the First World War it was partially excavated by Ernst Herzfeld and Friedrich Sarre, and more recently by the Iraq Department of Antiquities and British archaeologists. The material recovered from the site consists of magnificent carved stucco and painted panels, carved wood and tiles, as well as quantities of sherds. Much of it was subsequently divided among a number of different museums in Europe, North America and the Middle East.

The vast and rambling site of this unfinished ʿAbbasid capital, over 35 km long and situated nearly 100 km up the river Tigris from Baghdad, was built up in various stages during the ninth century. The Caliph al-Muʿtasim's motive for its foundation in AD 836 has been attributed to the desire to get away from Turkish troops who had been imported in vast numbers by a previous caliph, al-Ma'mun, in order to combat the Byzantines, and who had begun to cause increasing congestion and disorder in Baghdad. For the construction of the city, craftsmen and materials were brought from all over the empire and orders were sent for churches to be stripped of their columns and marble. Although Samarra was abandoned as the caliphal residence in AD 883, it continued to be occupied, according to the numismatic evidence, for at least a further century.

The surviving tiles come from various sectors of the palace of Jawsaq al-Khaqani and are of two principal types. The first are

11   plain green or yellow glazed tiles. It is possible that some of these may have been cut after firing and used for mosaic panels (on the reverse of some of the square tiles are guide marks for the cutter, and pieces of cut segments of tiles were also found). The second
–12 group are lustre and come from the harem and adjoining rooms, and include fragments of square tiles decorated with wreaths enclosing a cockerel as well as tiles with simple lustre flecks. These tiles are painted in vivid lustre colours – brilliant red and yellow – as well as more muted olive green and browns.

13   A reconstruction drawing by Sarre of the tile panels shows that the cockerel tiles were set at regular intervals surrounded by the plain flecked tiles. Confirming the eclectic nature of ʿAbbasid lustre ware designs, an interesting parallel has been drawn by Ettinghausen and Grabar between this design and those of third-century AD baked clay painted tiles from the ceiling of the House of Assembly in the synagogue of Dura-Europos in Syria, among which is a bird pecking fruit within a wreath. Other Samarra tile fragments – too small to make much sense of – seem to contain traces of inscriptions, with some bearing what are possibly craftsmen's signatures on the backs.

THE GREAT MOSQUE AT QAIROUAN

The Great Mosque at Qairouan south of Tunis is the second site at which ʿAbbasid lustre tiles have been found and, unlike Samarra, these are still in situ. Founded in AD 670 by the conqueror of North Africa, ʿUqba b. Nafiʿ, this mosque was destroyed and totally rebuilt by the Aghlabids, the governors of North Africa who became independent of the ʿAbbasids at the beginning of the ninth century. The reconstruction of the mosque began in AD 836 with major additions in 862 and 875. The 139 square lustre tiles
14   are set into the *mihrab* arch and walls on either side, to magnificent effect. The tradition concerning the installation of the tiles was described by the Arab chronicler Ibn Naji (d. AD 1494):

. . . for the work of the *mihrab*, they brought precious tiles intended for a reception hall which he [the amir] had wished to build, from Baghdad came teak wood for beams [also originally intended for the reception hall] and these were made into the *minbar* for the mosque. There also came pieces of marble for the *mihrab* from Iraq and these were assembled in the mosque and the tiles were placed on the face of the *mihrab*. A man from Baghdad made additional tiles and [the mosque] was decorated in this marvellous way with marble and gold and beautiful materials.

10 ABOVE Fragments of polychrome lustre earthenware tiles excavated from the Jawsaq al-Khaqani at Samarra, 9th century. Largest: 12×16 cm.

11 RIGHT Two fragments of monochrome yellow earthenware and one lustre tile from the Jawsaq al-Khaqani at Samarra. On the back of one of the yellow-glazed tiles (top right) cut marks are clearly visible. Largest: 8.5×7.5 cm.

12 Fragmentary lustre earthenware tile from the Jawsaq al-Khaqani, Samarra, 9th century. The motif of a bird within a wreath has parallels with 3rd-century AD baked clay tiles in the synagogue at Dura Europos. HT: 28 cm.

13 Reconstruction of tile panels excavated from the Jawsaq al-Khaqani at Samarra, 9th century. Plain lustre-flecked tiles were interspersed with the cockerel tiles. The lustre flecks may have been intended to imitate marble.

14 Lustre tiles in the
Great Mosque at
Qairouan, 9th century.
The designs include a
Sasanian crown, the
'peacock eye' motif and
pseudo-Arabic
calligraphy. Average
dimensions: 21.1 cm
each side.

Ibn Naji, writing some six centuries after the event, assumes the
Aghlabid amir responsible to have been Ziyadat Allah (AD
817–38), but it is thought more likely that the tiles date from the
middle rather than the early part of the ninth century.

The Qairouan tiles fall into two distinct stylistic groups. The
first are polychrome tiles with complex designs of medallions and
Sasanian-style winged palmettes. These motifs are found on
'Abbasid lustre vessels as well as on the stucco and woodwork
from Samarra. The monochrome tiles have much simpler designs
including geometric star patterns and schematised floral motifs.
Some of the tiles in this group have calligraphic designs, with
many of the words rendered quite illegibly. The bird-in-the-
wreath design of the Samarra tiles does not appear here. The polychrome tiles are the most prominently positioned in the mosque.
This suggests the possibility that the monochrome group of tiles
around the sides may have been those produced by the potter from
Baghdad mentioned by Ibn Naji.

There are still question marks hanging over the precise dating
of the 'Abbasid ceramics industry – 'Abbasid wares are still loosely

referred to as ninth to tenth century. There is also uncertainty about the location of the principal workshops. Attempts were made by Ernst Kühnel to suggest a firm dating for the lustre wares on the basis of the caliphal occupation of Samarra (AD 836–83). However, the further occupation of the city for another hundred years along with evidence from the Siraf excavations suggests that, while the tiles (at least those of Samarra) are likely to have been made during the caliphal occupation, other lustre wares may in fact have been produced well into the tenth century.

The technical consistency of the ʿAbbasid luxury wares means that either only one centre was responsible for their manufacture or, as with the pottery of Iznik five centuries later, the materials of production, the quality and the design were strictly controlled by the court. Unfortunately, the evidence from the wares themselves is scanty. Although at least a dozen different names have been collected from ʿAbbasid pottery, these are as simple as ʿamal (the work of) Abu'l Jaʿfar, telling us nothing about the craftsmen or where they came from.

Baghdad, Basra and Kufa are all possible centres of ceramic production during the ʿAbbasid period. Baghdad's claim rests entirely on Ibn Naji's reference in connection with the Qairouan tiles, although ceramic workshops would be expected in or near a capital city. For its part, Basra, on the river Tigris, was the most important ʿAbbasid commercial city and trading port of Iraq and a centre of glass manufacture. It is likely that Egyptian glass-makers brought the lustre technique here from Fustat (Old Cairo) and that the lustre technique was transferred to pottery at Basra.

In his account of the contruction of Samarra, the Arab chronicler Yaʿqubi describes how potters and glass-makers were brought to the site from Basra and says that potters also came from Kufa. These potters are likely to have set up temporary kilns in the city. In addition to this patchwork of documentary evidence there is recent petrographic analysis of sherds and kiln apparatus found at Basra (although the kilns themselves have not yet been located) and stored in the Metropolitan Museum of Art in New York. Comparisons of this material with sherds excavated at Siraf have shown the same composition of clays and glazes. Basra seems to be the most likely site, therefore, of sophisticated ceramic production for the region.

The ceramics industry of Iraq, whether based at Basra or elsewhere, began to wane during the latter part of the tenth century. Imitations of the metropolitan production continued to be made in many parts of the empire such as at Raqqa in northern Syria and Nishapur in eastern Iran. An important centre of lustre produc-

15 Fragmentary tile in the Museum of Islamic Art in Cairo, probably made at Fustat, with green glaze and sgraffito design of a rabbit, *c.*11th century.

tion was established in Egypt at Fustat under the Fatimids (AD 969–1171), but as in Iraq the emphasis was evidently on the production of vessels. Very few tiles have been recovered from excavations and these are decorated in sgraffito technique (incised underglaze designs).

There is, however, a small but significant group of lustre tiles from North Africa produced during the eleventh century. The most important of these were found at the site of Qal'at Bani Hammad in Algeria, a royal complex of palaces, a mosque and a magnificent tower, begun *c.* AD 1050, and built by a Berber dynasty. The tiles are painted in lustre with stylised epigraphic motifs in Kufic script, the ends of the letters often extended upwards into foliate terminals. The repeated phrases generally contain standard words of good wishes, such as *barakah* (blessing) or *yumn* (prosperity). However, as with the epigraphy on the Qairouan tiles, the words are sometimes so schematised that they have simply become design. An interesting feature of these fragmentary tiles is that they are cruciform, intended to form a panel with eight-pointed tiles, and thus coincidentally anticipate the thirteenth-century tiles of Kashan in Iran.

In the next chapter we shall see how, from these hesitant early beginnings, the use of tilework for interiors was to increase dramatically. Fascination continued with the shimmering tones of the lustre pigments, and lustre tiles become an important feature of architectural decoration. In the hands of the great potting families of Kashan they were to reach an unparalleled degree of virtuosity and sophistication.

16 Fragmentary lustre cross tiles from the Qal'at b. Hammad in Algeria, 11th century. Largest: 6×12 cm.

—3—

AN EXPLOSION OF
TILES

IRAN, ANATOLIA

AND SYRIA

12TH—14TH CENTURIES

The Seljuq and Il-Khanid periods mark the first of the great eras of Islamic tilework. Experimentation and innovation took place in a whole range of ceramic techniques under both these dynasties and vast numbers of tiles survive, many with dates and craftsmen's signatures. In addition, extensive religious patronage by both the rulers and the religious élite resulted in the building of numerous funerary monuments and shrines, the most important of which were decorated with lustre tiles.

The historical picture opens with the reign of the Great Seljuqs. Of Turkish origin, they ruled Iraq and Iran between AD 1038 and 1194, with separate branches ruling in Syria and Kirman. Although, ironically, the beginning of this surge of artistic activity seems to have occurred only in the last days of Seljuq rule, this highly productive period continued well after the Seljuq empire had split up into smaller entities. The Seljuq line itself continued only in Anatolia (see page 57). In Baghdad the ʿAbbasid caliphs, already in decline, reasserted themselves, but it was not long before they (and the whole Islamic world) were thrown into confusion by the invasions of the Mongols who took Baghdad, the seat of the empire, in AD 1258. Once established, the Il-Khanid Mongol dynasty (AD 1256–1353) was even more prolific in its artistic patronage than the Seljuqs; new monuments were built throughout Iran and tile production increased accordingly.

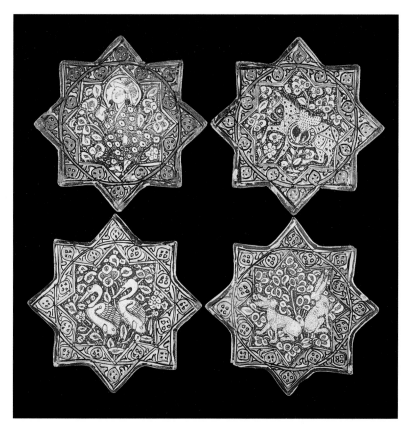

17 Eight-pointed star tiles, stone-paste, opaque white glaze, underglaze cobalt blue borders, overglaze lustre, 13th century. The crossover garment and plumed hat of the figure (top left) is typical of the Mongol garb commonly depicted on Kashan lustre. Average DIAM: 21 cm.

KASHAN

The principal centre for the production of fine pottery and tile-work was the town of Kashan in central Iran, which gave its name to the Persian word for tile (*kashi*). Although there were doubtless other potteries functioning in Iran in the medieval period, evidence of Kashan's pre-eminent position between the twelfth and fourteenth centuries comes additionally from the signatures of a number of well-known potters, the most famous of whom were members of the Abu Tahir family, who signed their names on tiles and vessels. Some added their *nisbah* (place of origin) 'Kashani' next to their signature or stated, as in a tile in the British Museum dated AH 739/AD 1339, that they resided in Kashan.

The geographer Yaqut, writing in the thirteenth century, mentions the export of Kashan's ceramics, and although the area has not been systematically excavated, finds of wasters (objects spoiled in the kiln) and the remains of kilns have been made in the area. Dated pieces abound for this period; the earliest known so far is a small jar in the British Museum dated AH 575/AD 1179-80. Dates on surviving tiles indicate that the tile production of Kashan

35

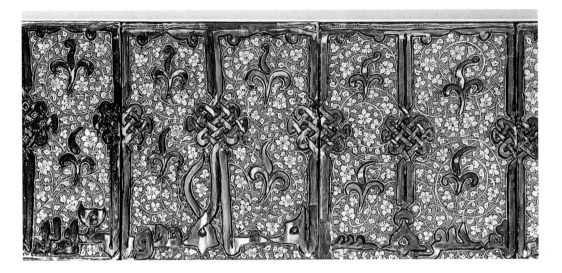

18 ABOVE Frieze of four lustre tiles with moulded Kufic Qur'anic inscription, 'the merciful, the compassionate, there is no God but he, the mighty, the wise' (*surah* 3). Late 13th–14th century. Each tile: 141×57 cm.

20 OPPOSITE, BELOW Five-pointed star tile with flat base, stone-paste, opaque white glaze, overglaze lustre, 13th century. This unusually shaped tile probably fitted along the bottom row of a dado panel. The *naskhi* Arabic inscription around the margin is from Qur'an *surah* 3, v. 26–7, with the additional phrase 'the mighty God spoke the truth as did his Prophet'. DIAM: 31 cm.

continued almost without a break from just after AD 1200 to the 1330s.

The Mongol invasions caused only a brief hiccup in the tile industry of Kashan – there are no dated tiles between 1243 and 1255 – but not the total destruction suffered by the potteries of Afrasiyab, the old city of Samarqand in Central Asia, or Raqqa on the Euphrates. The same techniques and styles continued in use on tilework after the Mongol invasions and developed ever more interesting forms, with tiles and vessels (so-called Sultanabad ware) produced from about the 1270s distinguished from earlier ones by the introduction of chinoiserie motifs.

Shrines and palaces

The production of Kashan tiles was obviously immense and since the turn of this century tiles (mostly without provenance) have been constantly on the art market and avidly collected. Enough tiles still survive in situ, however, to indicate the type of buildings that were tiled. These were largely funerary monuments, in particular those devoted specifically to the Shiite sect. The Shiites, who were sometimes persecuted under the Seljuq Sunnis, enjoyed much greater freedom of worship under the Mongol Il-Khanids. Their most important shrines were at Qumm, Najaf and Mashhad, but other towns (including Kashan itself) were also significant Shiite centres.

The tiles produced throughout most of the thirteenth century are decorated with both figural and non-figural motifs. They frequently have inscriptions in the cursive *naskhi* script around their borders that include Persian poetry, verses from the Qur'an 19,2 31,3

19 ABOVE Star and cross lustre tiles, from a group of about 160 tiles originally in the Imamzadeh Yahya at Veramin, made between October and December AD 1262 (AH 660–1). Qur'anic Arabic inscriptions in *naskhi* script (left to right): *surah* 2, v. 255, dated Dhu'l Hijjah 660/*surah* 36, v. 22–8, dated 660/*surah* 33, v. 56, *surah* 97 (all), dated Safar 661/*surah* 3, v. 190–2/*surah* 1 (all), *surah* 18, v. 110, dated Safar 661/*surah* 76, v. 11–17/*surah* 1 (all), *surah* 112 (all)/*surah* 2, v. 255, dated Dhu'l Hijjah 660. Average DIAM: 31 cm.

21 Eight-pointed star and cross tiles, stone-paste, opaque white glaze, underglaze cobalt blue and turquoise (on the star tiles), overglaze lustre. These are thought to belong to a group, a number of which are dated AH 664–5/ AD 1266–7, once in the Imamzadeh Ja'far at Damghan. The Persian inscriptions in *naskhi* script consist of verses of poetry from the *Shahnameh*. DIAM (each tile): 20.1 cm.

or (rarely) pseudo-inscriptions. While it is likely that the figural 31 tiles were largely destined for secular use, with non-figural tiles intended for religious contexts, it is clear that some figural tiles were used in the Shiite shrines. The growing association of Shiism and Sufism in medieval Iran would have made the use of love poetry in a shrine perfectly acceptable as, in the Sufi tradition, human love could be used as an allegory for divine love. The British Museum's star and cross tiles, with designs of animals and 21 Persian quatrains in the margins, are thought to be part of a group that once covered the walls of the Imamzadeh Ja'far in Damghan, dated AD 1267. The depiction of living beings in a religious context was not, however, universally approved. The monumental tiles from the shrine of 'Abd al-Samad (AD 1307) have birds in the background of the Qur'anic inscription. All the tiles known from this group have had the heads of the birds knocked off, presumably while they were still in situ.

Palaces, too, were decorated with tiles, which can be seen

58

clearly in the background decorations of miniature paintings of the *Shahnameh* (Book of Kings). The only secular structure from the Il-Khanid period to have survived and been thoroughly excavated is Takht-i Sulayman, the Il-Khanid palace of Abaqa Khan, built during the 1270s in the province of Persian Azerbaijan south of Tabriz. The palace, constructed on the site of a Zoroastrian temple, is an important source for the study of Iranian tilework of the Il-Khanid period. That at least some of the tiles were made on the site is evident from the finds of kilns and tile moulds. It is not yet clear, however, whether monochrome only or lustre tiles as well were produced there. The site has yielded fragments in addition to complete star and cross tiles (including some animal cross tiles virtually identical to those from Damghan) and monumental

22,29 frieze tiles, many of which are now scattered among various museums. With figural or floral designs, the tiles are mostly painted in lustre but with a significant proportion in *lajvardina*. A number of tiles bear dates, generally in the AH 670s/AD 1270s.

One of the most interesting aspects of these tiles is their inscriptions. They are often religious in nature with verses from the Qur'an, or with references to Shiite imams. A second group,

22 Rectangular tile, stone-paste, opaque white glaze, overglaze lustre. The moulded Persian *naskhi* inscription from the *Shahnameh* is picked out in underglaze blue. On either side of the arch outlined in turquoise are animal heads growing out of a tree. This tile is part of a series with similar decoration from Takht-i Sulayman, datable to the 1270s. 29.7×30.3 cm.

23 Hexagonal tile, stone-paste, turquoise glaze with Kufic inscription 'the Merciful', one of the 99 names of Allah. Late 12th—13th century. DIAM: 20 cm.

24 Rectangular tile, stone-paste, turquoise glaze, late 12th—13th century. This tile in the shape of a small *mihrab* has a moulded *naskhi* inscription in cobalt from the Qur'an, *surah* 112. 19.7×14.7 cm.

however, contains verses from the *Shahnameh*, the Persian national epic recited and illustrated since its composition by the writer Firdawsi in AD 1010. It was composed in Persian, in verse, and contains stories of adventure and heroism from Iran's ancient past. Asadullah Souren Melikian-Chirvani has argued that the choice of inscriptions on these tiles is highly significant: the Shiite references deliberately state the Il-Khanids' religious orientation, while the *Shahnameh* verses, in addition to the choice of an historic site for the location of the palace, elicit comparison between its builder, Abaqa Khan, and the great Achaemenid or Sasanian rulers.

Techniques and designs

The large number of surviving Kashan lustre tiles and the interest shown in them by Western scholars because of their inscriptions and iconography tend to obscure the fact that lustre tiles were only a fairly small and exclusive part of the tile production of this period, the bulk of which was mostly monochrome tilework in
23 turquoise or blue. Among the blue tiles in the British Museum
24 collection is a delightful example in the shape of a *mihrab*. A number of other techniques were also used, namely underglaze painting and the overglaze techniques of *minai* and *lajvardina*.

Minai tiles produced in the first half of the thirteenth century were evidently only used on a small number of buildings: they are more frequently associated with Anatolia (see page 59). *Minai* was sometimes combined with lustre, as in a rare example in the Museum of Fine Arts in Boston. *Minai* was replaced in the last
25–9 quarter of the century by *lajvardina*, many more tiles of which survive. They are characterised by a cobalt or turquoise ground with overglaze gilding. The appearance of *lajvardina* tiles at
67 Takht-i Sulayman provides a date for the production of this type in the 1270s. The technique was still in use a century later on tiles
69 in the funerary complex of the Shah-i Zindah at Samarqand.

Cobalt blue or turquoise underglaze painting is frequently found combined with Kashan lustre, both on the star tiles and emphasising inscriptions on larger frieze tiles. Underglaze-painted tiles without lustre include tiles painted in blue and black and tiles with relief-moulded inscriptions and chinoiserie designs in blue-and-white. Examples still in situ are found in the tomb of Uljaitu (d. 1307) at Sultaniyah and, from the latter half of the fourteenth
69 century, in Samarqand at the Shah-i Zindah complex.

Evidence that the same potters were producing both pots and tiles in different techniques and in the same workshops is clearly demonstrated by the work of the prolific potter Abu Zaid, who

25 Fragments of monochrome blue and *lajvardina* tiles, stone-paste, painted over a turquoise glaze in red, cobalt blue and gold, 13th century. Part of a group collected by Sir Percy Sykes in Herat in 1902. Largest: 8 cm.

26 RIGHT Fragmentary *lajvardina mihrab*, stone-paste, painted over a cobalt glaze in gold and red, second half of 13th century. The moulded inscription around the side is from the Qur'an, *surah* 41, v. 30–1. In the centre beneath the lobed arch is the name of the deceased Jalal al-Din Isma'il, his honorific titles and antecedents. Base: 38.5×59 cm; top: 43.5×34 cm.

28 OPPOSITE, LEFT Rectangular *lajvardina* tile, stone-paste, painted over a turquoise glaze in red and gold, second half of 13th century. The Kufic inscription is probably Qur'anic. 35.2×16 cm.

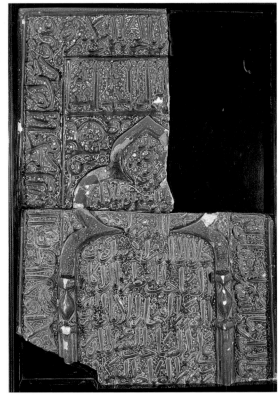

27 Star and cross *lajvardina* tiles, stone-paste, painted over a turquoise and cobalt ground with chinoiserie lotus flowers on long stalks in red and gold, second half of 13th century. Average W: 20 cm.

29 BELOW Rectangular *lajvardina* frieze tile, stone-paste, painted over a cobalt glaze in red and gold, second half of 13th century. Moulded Persian inscription reading 'the kingdom of the world' in the centre and chinoiserie phoenix and a dragon in a band along the top. 45×51 cm.

was also a poet and inscribed some of his poetry on the tiles. At least fifteen lustre and *minai* vessels and tiles signed by him are so far known, dated between AH 587/AD 1191 and AH 616/AD 1219. One of the best examples of his work is a star-shaped tile in the Museum of Fine Arts in Boston, which depicts a figure mounted on horseback hunting with his dog, the countryside represented by a cypress tree and a dense array of birds. 33

In the genre scenes, which continue to appear on star tiles for well over a century, the human figures conform to a common physical type representing Persian ideals of beauty. With their moon faces, long narrow eyes, joined eyebrows and long thick locks of hair, they reflect the stylised Turkic features of the Seljuq and Mongol invaders. These physical characteristics are also common to figural scenes in contemporary metalwork (such as the Blacas ewer in the British Museum, made in Mosul in 1232), thirteenth-century wall paintings, and miniature paintings of the fourteenth century. 17,3 33–

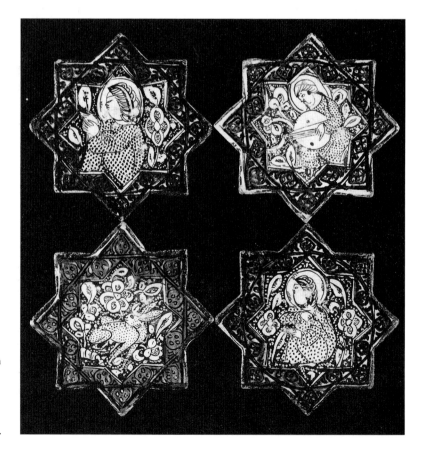

30 Eight-pointed star tiles, stone-paste, opaque white glaze, underglaze cobalt blue borders, overglaze lustre. The female figures are depicted in profile holding objects whose function is not clear. One has what is possibly a bowl in both hands, the other a ribbon(?) in her left hand; the turbanned man is playing a lute. Average DIAM: 12.5 cm.

31 Star tile, stone-paste, opaque white glaze and overglaze lustre. Around the border is a pseudo-Arabic inscription. 13th–14th century. DIAM: 10.5 cm.

32 Star tile, stone-paste, opaque white glaze and overglaze lustre. Qur'anic inscription around the border is *surah* 110, v. 1–3. On the back (fig. 39) is a painted figure of an archer. 13th century. DIAM: 22.5 cm.

33 Eight-pointed star tile, stone-paste, opaque white glaze, overglaze lustre, painted by the potter Abu Zaid. The Persian *naskhi* inscription includes poetry by Abu'l Faraj Runi and the phrase 'written by Abu Zaid in his own hand in Rabi` II 608' (September 1211). DIAM: 28.5 cm.

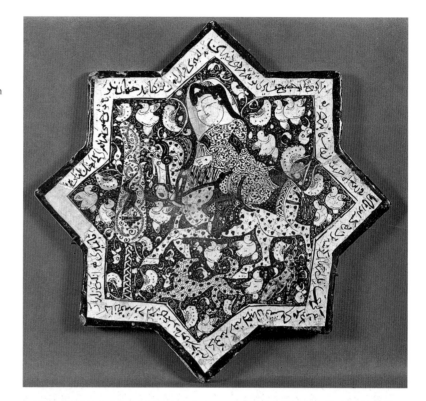

34 Eight-pointed star tile, stone-paste, opaque white glaze, underglaze cobalt and turquoise, overglaze lustre, late 13th–14th century. The *naskhi* Persian inscription, which consists of verses of Persian love poetry, includes the lines: 'Last night the moon came to your house, filled with envy I thought of chasing him away. Who is the moon to sit in the same place as you?' DIAM: 20.5 cm.

36 ABOVE Back of tile (fig. 35, left) with a seal impression in *nasta'liq* script of a later owner of the tile, 'Ali b. Husayn Akbar, and the date AH 1240/ AD 1824–5.

35 LEFT Eight-pointed star tile, stone-paste, opaque white glaze, underglaze turquoise and cobalt and overglaze lustre. The Persian inscriptions in *naskhi* consist of verses of poetry, the date AH 739/AD 1339, and the statement that it was made in Kashan. Following this in Arabic is the phrase 'May God protect it from the vicissitudes of time'. The base has been broken off and replaced by a fragment from another tile on which are the beginnings of a verse from the *Shahnameh*. DIAM: 21.5 cm.

While for the most part the scenes painted on the Kashan tiles are simply genre scenes and do not represent a particular story, the verses of Persian poetry inscribed around their borders bearing little relationship to the subject, an exception is a tile in the Keir collection. This depicts a recognisable scene from the Bizhan and Manizha cycle in the *Shahnameh*, in which Bizhan is rescued from a dungeon by the epic hero Rustam. This tile, like the *minai* beaker in the Freer Gallery of Art in Washington, DC which is also painted with a series of scenes from the same *Shahnameh* cycle, inevitably invites the question of whether the potters were copying book illustrations to reproduce the scenes from the story. The difficulty is that, apart from the Varqa and Gulshah manuscript in the Topkapi Saray produced in the mid thirteenth century, no other illustrated Persian manuscripts contemporary with this pottery are yet known. Whether they were produced and have not survived, or whether book illustration had not developed is not clear at this point. If the potters did not use manuscript illustration for inspiration, then wall paintings (such as the fragment in the Metropolitan Museum of Art illustrated here) produced at this time, in a tradition going back to the magnificent Central Asian

37

41

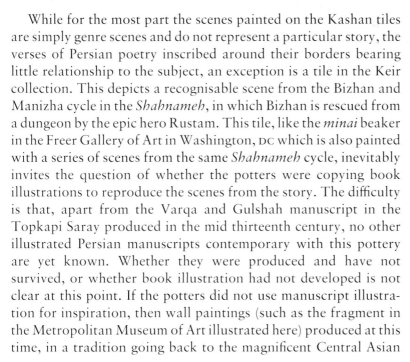

37 Rectangular lustre tile, 13th century, with scene from the *Shahnameh*, showing Rustam lifting the rock from the entrance to the cave in which Bihzan has been imprisoned. The Persian inscription reads 'the coming of Rustam to the top of the pit'. 30.4×30.2 cm.

Sogdian paintings of the seventh and eighth centuries, may have been a possible source. This is a view argued by Mariana Shreve Simpson.

A curious feature shared by two tiles, one in the British Museum and the other in the Metropolitan Museum of Art in New York, is that there appear to be preparatory sketches for figural tiles drawn in lustre on the backs, one an archer on horseback (similar to the archer depicted in the middle of a battle scene on a dish in the Freer Gallery, shown here) and the other a seated figure (on the back of a tile dated AH 663/AD 1265). The fronts of both have stylised floral decoration.

39–4

38

32

38 PREVIOUS PAGE, ABOVE Detail of a stone-paste *mina'i* dish, early 13th century, showing an archer in similar stance to the drawing on the back of the lustre tile (fig. 39).

39 & 40 PREVIOUS PAGE, BELOW Sketches on the backs of lustre tiles. The tile on the left (see fig. 32) has an archer, the tile on the right a seated figure (the front is dated AH 663/ AD 1265).

From the shrine at Mashhad, dated AH 612/AD 1215, one of the earliest surviving buildings in Iran with tiles, it is clear that both star tiles and large frieze tiles were produced at the same time and were considered from the very beginning to be integral elements of a single scheme. In this building, the lustre star tiles (signed by Abu Zaid) interspersed with plain turquoise tiles form a dado panel around the walls and are surmounted by inscriptional frieze tiles some 45 cm high. Many more large frieze tiles survive, however, from the late thirteenth/early fourteenth century, and a characteristic format can be seen, particularly on tiles associated with Takht-i Sulayman or the shrine of 'Abd al-Samad at Natanz. They are divided into three fields, the central one usually bearing an inscription moulded in relief that is Qur'anic or secular in nature, and picked out in cobalt or turquoise. Like the tiles in Mashhad, the upper border continues to be decorated with moulded plant motifs, while the narrow lower segment contains a border of squiggles resembling an inscription.

A singular achievement of the Kashan potters was to create large *mihrabs* made up of tiles of different shapes. One of the most impressive is the *mihrab* (now in the Islamic Museum in Berlin) of the Masjid-i Maydan at Kashan, signed by al-Hasan ibn 'Arab-shah and dated AH 623/AD 1226. Like the cenotaph of the Imam Jalal al-Din 'Ali in the British Museum, the decoration is dense, the lustre enhanced by touches of blue and turquoise on the inscription.

Tiles made during the latter half of the thirteenth century bear chinoiserie designs. The earliest examples of these motifs, found both in lustre and in *lajvardina*, come from Takht-i Sulayman and are dated between AD 1271 and 1275. While the influence of China had already been felt earlier in the history of Islamic ceramics in the attempts to copy the fabric and forms of Tang and Song porcelain, the close contacts between China and the Islamic world under the Il-Khanids (a cadet branch of the Mongol Yuan dynasty ruling China) resulted in Chinese wares being carried west along the various maritime and Central Asian trade routes so that they were widely available in the markets of the Middle East.

The Chinese designs disseminated through objects, particularly Chinese silks, were to provide a wealth of new sources of inspiration, and Far Eastern animal and flower motifs began to pervade all forms of Islamic art. The *lajvardina* and lustre tiles as well as the late thirteenth-century Sultanabad vessels and tiles of this period are decorated with lotus flowers, dragons and phoenixes. Another popular motif on Il-Khanid pottery was the flying crane – in China a symbol of good fortune and longevity – although we

43

18,2

43–7

43,4

48

49

41 ABOVE Wall painting, early 13th century. In the upper register are standing or kneeling figures, and in the lower are two horsemen killing a snake. Their features and costumes are depicted in the same manner as on Kashan tiles (see fig. 42). W: 60.32 cm.

42 LEFT Kashan tile with seated figure, 13th century. DIAM: 13.5 cm.

43 OPPOSITE Lustre tiles in situ in the shrine at Mashhad, showing how star and frieze tiles were used together. The star tiles are signed by the Kashan potter Abu Zaid and dated AH 612/AD 1215. HT (frieze tiles): *c*.45 cm.

44 LEFT Rectangular tile, stone-paste, opaque white glaze with underglaze turquoise and blue. The moulded Qur'anic Arabic inscription is from *surah* 76, v. 9. About 20 tiles from this frieze, from the shrine of 'Abd al-Samad at Natanz, survive; one in the Metropolitan Museum of Art is dated AH 707/AD 1307–8. In all cases the heads of the birds have been knocked off. 35.8×36.8 cm.

45 LEFT Rectangular frieze tile, stone-paste, opaque white glaze, underglaze blue and turquoise, overglaze lustre. The moulded Persian inscription is from the *Shahnameh*. Late 13th–14th century. 29×31 cm.

46 Rectangular frieze tile, stone-paste, opaque white glaze, overglaze lustre, late 13th–14th century. The moulded inscription picked out in cobalt blue, 'bin [son of] Ja'far bin Muhammad', refers to a son of Ja'far al-Sadiq (d. AD 765, one of the 8th-century Shiite imams, himself son of Imam Muhammad al-Baqir, d. *c.* AD 737). 40×42 cm.

47 Rectangular frieze tile, stone-paste, opaque white glaze, overglaze lustre. The moulded *naskhi* inscription picked out in cobalt bears the date Sha'ban 709 (January 1310). A band of chinoiserie lotus blossoms stained in underglaze cobalt runs along the top, and there are turquoise splashes on the ground. The rest of the frieze, of which there are two further tiles in the British Museum, contains Qur'anic inscriptions. 39×42.7 cm.

48 Two rectangular tiles, stone-paste, opaque white glaze, overglaze lustre, first half of 14th century. The panel in the shape of a *mihrab*, with pilasters in turquoise, is a tombstone inscribed with the name of the deceased Qadi Jalal al-Din ʿAli. The inscriptions in *naskhi* script, picked out in underglaze blue, consist of his name and honorific title *malik al-ʿulama* (king of the learned men) with his genealogy going back through seven generations of *qadi*s. The Qurʾanic verse along the outer edge is from *surah* 2, v. 255–6. HT: 131 cm.

49 & 50 Eight-pointed star tiles, stone-paste, opaque white glaze, underglaze cobalt and overglaze lustre, 14th century. The chinoiserie designs of flying cranes and lotus flowers are painted in white slip, characteristic of the so-called Sultanabad style. The tile on the right bears the date AH 729/AD 1328. Average DIAM: 21 cm.

cannot know whether the Islamic patrons and craftsmen understood this or simply liked the design. The fact that these designs appear at Takht-i Sulayman, however, does suggest that these Chinese motifs had become a recognised and important element of the Mongol court style, demonstrating their eastern links.

By the mid fourteenth century the great potteries of Kashan were in decline; the lustre technique did not die, however, and isolated examples of lustre tiles have been documented between the fourteenth and seventeenth centuries. There are particularly fine examples from the reign of the Timurid Sultan Abu Saʿid (AD 1451–69). In the seventeenth century the manufacture of lustre was actively revived, but largely for use on vessels. The only examples of Safavid lustre tiles known so far are two fragments, possibly from a water course (one each in the British Museum and the Victoria and Albert Museum), painted in the feathery style found on contemporary lustre vessels. Later in the nineteenth century, Iranian potters began producing revivalist lustre tiles in the style of Kashan.

THE EASTERN ISLAMIC WORLD

The production of lustre tiles appears to have been limited to Kashan or to potters from Kashan who were called to work on specific monuments elsewhere. In the eastern part of the Islamic world we find other kinds of tiles produced for interior use. At

51 ABOVE Lustre tile fragment from the side of a water course, stone-paste, opaque white glaze, overglaze lustre, 17th century. It is painted on both sides with birds and plants. According to an ink inscription in English on the side of the tile, it was found 'on the plain between Murchikhurt between Kashan and Isfahan'. 10.5×17×4.3 cm.

52 BELOW Lustre tile, stone-paste, opaque white glaze, overglaze lustre, 19th century. The Arabic inscription in *naskhi* script reads 'the kingdom belongs to Allah the mighty, the just(?) the only one'. 19×33 cm.

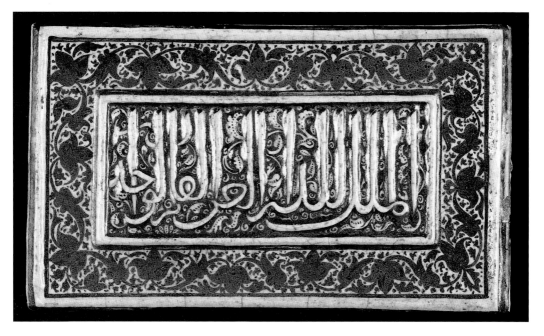

53 Brown glazed tile, stone-paste, moulded, early 13th century. This tile is part of a group excavated from the palace of Mas'ud III at Ghazni, which was occupied until 1221 when it was destroyed during the Mongol invasions. 10.5×10.5 cm.

Ghazni, the capital of the Ghaznavid rulers of Afghanistan (AD 977–1186), an interesting group of moulded tiles glazed in mono- **53** chrome colours was excavated from the palace of Mas'ud III (AD 1099–1115). The tiles are decorated in a variety of animal, arabesque and epigraphic motifs, some with dotted borders, which hark back to pre-Islamic Iranian motifs. The animals – lions, gazelles and mythical beasts – are portrayed singly in a static heraldic stance. Quantities of carved glazed bowls from the site of Shahr-i Gholgola near Bamiyan, destroyed by the Mongols in 1221, have clear, turquoise glazes or sgraffito decoration and confirm that pottery vessels were produced in the medieval period in Afghanistan. The Ghazni palace tiles are unique, however, and are likely to have been made on site specifically for the palace.

Stone-paste inscriptional tiles have been found in excavations at Nishapur dating to the twelfth century, while glazed terracotta **54** tiles for both interior and exterior use, intricately carved with inscriptions and flora and geometric ornament, were produced for a short period during the latter half of the fourteenth century. The discussion of these tiles, which are found at various sites in Central Asia along with *cuerda seca* tiles and tile mosaic, fits more appropriately in the next chapter. At Saray Berke, capital of the Golden

54 Fragment of inscription frieze tile, possibly Qur'anic, stone-paste, carved and turquoise glazed, 12th century. Found during the excavations of the Metropolitan Museum of Art at Nishapur in 1936. 27.9×25.4 cm.

Horde whose Khanate (AD 1226–1502) lay to the north of the Caspian and Black seas, there was a flourishing pottery industry during the fourteenth century producing wares linked to the Sultanabad group. These and numerous tiles excavated from the site, painted under the glaze and in the *lajvardina* style, are in the Hermitage Museum in St Petersburg. Saray Berke was described by the geographer al-'Umari (d. AD 1349) as having 'innumerable ateliers, tile and pottery workshops and high kilns'.

SELJUQ ANATOLIA AND SYRIA

In the mid eleventh century Seljuq Turks, assisted by bands of Turkmen, began their incursions into the Byzantine-held territories of Anatolia. A major defeat of the Byzantine armies in AD 1071 at the battle of Manzikert led, a few years later, to the establishment of the state of the Seljuqs of Rum, whose capital was at Konya. The civilisation reached its apogee during the first half of the thirteenth century with a prosperity based on the commercial advantages of the capture of the ports of Sinope (AD 1215) on the Black Sea and Antalya (AD 1226) on the Mediterranean.

55 Tile mosaic in blue and black from Konya, first half of 13th century, now in the Victoria and Albert Museum.

A great burst of architectural activity during the thirteenth and fourteenth centuries has left a large number of important monuments – mosques, *madrasahs* (religious colleges), tombs and palaces in the principal towns of Anatolia, Konya, Beyşehir, Sivas and others. It is here that the elaborate and time-consuming technique of cut tilework was developed and used to magnificent effect. The most stunning examples are in the interiors of religious buildings where they are clothing walls, *mihrabs* and domes. The designs include a combination of grand geometric patterns, arabesques and highly elaborate inscriptional panels, usually in a characteristic colour scheme of turquoise and black. From Anatolia, the technique of tile mosaic spread back to Iran where it was extensively used in the Timurid monuments of the fourteenth and fifteenth centuries, as we shall see in the following chapter.

Tilework was also widely used in the Anatolian palaces. In

contrast to tile mosaic, these tiles clearly show the influence of the potteries of Kashan. In the pavilion of Qilij Arslan II (AD 1156–92) at Konya, for instance, star and cross tiles have been found decorated in the overglaze *minai* technique, some with arabesque and others with figural designs. *Minai* tiles from Iran do exist, as mentioned above, but they are extremely rare and these examples are close both in style and technique to the contemporary *minai* bowls produced at the Kashan potteries. Excavations at the idyllically situated Kubadabad palace, built by ʿAla al-Din Kaykubad (AD 1219–37) on the shore of Lake Beyşehir, have revealed tiles in the throne room, the *diwan* and various adjoining rooms. These include the banqueting hall which the chronicler Ibn Bibi described as the place where 'music was played and wine was drunk'. These tiles depict birds, animals and delightful turbanned figures, painted in underglaze and in lustre. The style of painting of these Anatolian tiles, particularly the large scale of the designs and their loosely drawn background plant ornaments, is strikingly similar to that of the ceramics of Raqqa. Evidence from the site suggests that the tiles were made in situ and it is likely that Syrian potters were involved in their production.

The Euphrates potteries centred on Raqqa were active from the last quarter of the twelfth century until the city was destroyed by the Mongol invaders in the mid thirteenth century. Influenced to a great extent by Kashan but with a spirit and style entirely their own, they produced a wide variety of stone-paste pottery that included underglaze painted vessels in black with transparent or turquoise glazes, polychrome underglaze wares in a style that imitated the designs found on Kashan *minai* ware, and lustre. The focus of the Raqqa production was on vessels. Tiles were produced, but not in great quantities; figural lustre tiles in the style of Kashan and a few underglaze painted tiles have recently been recovered during the excavation of the later twelfth/early thirteenth-century palace known as Qasr al-Banat.

In the next chapter we shall look at the changes that took place in the tilework of Iran from the late fourteenth century onwards and look further to Central Asia. The tilework discussed so far, primarily decorated with lustre, had been destined for internal use, with its main purpose the embellishment of key places in the interiors of the buildings such as the *mihrab*. The next chapter deals with tiles made for external use, where the approach is very different: the subtle lustre tones give way to walls of brilliant colour in the new techniques of tile mosaic and *cuerda seca*. The ceramic vessel and tile industries, so intimately linked during this period, now diverge.

56 ABOVE Detail of underglaze painted stone-paste tile from the Kubadabad palace at Beyşehir.

57 RIGHT Fragmentary stone-paste lustre tile from Qasr al-Banat at Raqqa, 12th–13th century.

58 OPPOSITE Rustam striking the door of Afrasiyab's palace, from a Safavid *Shahnameh*, Isfahan, c.1610. 15.4×22.7 cm. The façade of the palace is decorated with panels of tiles, and the brickwork itself is highlighted with glazed blue plugs.

— 4 —

VEILS OF
SPLENDOUR

IRAN AND CENTRAL ASIA
14TH–19TH CENTURIES

Timur (AD 1370–1405), or Tamerlane as he is also known, claiming his descent from the Mongol Chingiz Khan, despite being of Turkish origin, emerged as ruler of the previously Chagatayid domains of Central Asia during the last quarter of the fourteenth century. From his base in Transoxania he conquered Iran, expelled the Muzaffarids from Fars and the Jalayirids from Iraq. He defeated the Ottoman sultan Bayezid at the battle of Ankara, sacked Delhi, and his campaigns in Russia took him to within 350 km of Moscow. Samarqand, close to the ancient site of Afrasiyab, became the capital of his vast empire.

TIMURIDS

Timur is famous both for his extraordinary cruelty and for his great artistic patronage; his conquests involved massacres of general populations while artisans were carried off from all parts of his new empire to the principal Timurid cities and in particular to Samarqand. Vast architectural projects, palaces, mausolea and mosques were commissioned by him and his successors. Eight structures survive that were built by Timur, while a further twenty-five are documented in the literary sources. It was just after overseeing the construction of great formal gardens in his capital, and while planning a campaign against China, that he died in Utrar in 1405 and was buried in the Gur-i Mir at Samarqand.

Our most evocative descriptions of Timur and his court come from the Spanish ambassador Ruy Gonzales de Clavijo, who was in Samarqand a year before Timur's death. Clavijo describes the city of Samarqand as bustling with merchants; shortly before he got there a caravan of 800 camels had arrived, bearing merchandise from China. During his stay he witnessed great building activity, marvelling at the speed – a mere twenty days – with which a bazaar was erected. Timur himself, Clavijo says, personally supervised the building of his Friday mosque the 'Bibi Khanum' and would come every day, despite his failing health, to urge on the work, throwing pieces of meat and coins down to the workmen to encourage them. The picture Clavijo paints is one of fantastic opulence, with beautiful pavilions and palaces set in lovely gardens, and he remarked particuarly on the lavish use of blue and gold tiles everywhere. The building that impressed him most was the Aq Saray, Timur's palace at the city of Shahr-i Sabz, his birthplace and second capital:

61

From this main portal . . . you enter a great reception hall which is a room four square, where the walls are panelled with gold and blue tiles, and the ceiling is entirely of gold work. From this room we were taken into the galleries, and in these likewise everywhere the walls were of gilt tiles. We saw indeed here so many apartments and separate chambers, all of which were adorned in tilework of blue and gold with many other colours, that it would take too long to describe them here, and all were so marvellously wrought that even the craftsmen of Paris, who are so noted for their skill, would hold that which is done here to be of very fine workmanship.

All that still stands of the Aq Saray, built between 1379 and 1396, is its massive entrance portal. Never completed, it was still under construction when Clavijo saw it. The palace was probably built with the assistance of Khwarazmian craftsmen brought by Timur from the sacked city of Kunya Urgench, in addition to craftsmen from Tabriz. It remains, particularly from the point of view of tile-work, arguably one of the most important Timurid monuments.

The style of Timurid architecture grew out of the Il-Khanid tradition of brick architecture. Monumentality was the aim – high portals, vast arched *iwans* (vaulted halls open at one end) and turquoise domes that stood out like beacons. They were lavishly decorated, many with painted ceilings in addition to tilework. The Timurid artists and craftsmen, many of whom had come from far afield, created an intricate decorative style characterised by a subtle blend of Chinese and traditional Islamic motifs, often described as the international Timurid style (its effect on the art of the Ottomans will be discussed in the next chapter). Within this general style, however, distinct regional variations can be observed. For instance, some designs look more Persian, others more Central Asian. These can probably be attributed to the provenance of the artists involved. The existence of a 'court style' is emphasised by a passage from the *arza dasht*, an important document written in the second half of the fifteenth century and now in the Topkapi Palace library. Listing work in progress in a Timurid scriptorium, it refers to a certain Khwaja ʿAbd al-Rahim, who is noted as being 'busy making designs for binders, illuminators, tentmakers and tile cutters'. Michael Rogers has argued that this refers particularly to patterns with central designs and corner pieces, which would have been suitable for (and are indeed found on) depictions of tents, manuscript illumination and tiles.

Techniques and designs

Whereas during the Seljuq and Il-Khanid periods the same techniques and designs on the whole were being used to decorate both vessels and tiles, the industries now diverged. Timurid period pottery vessels are generally decorated in blue-and-white designs inspired by Chinese blue-and-white porcelain. The tilemakers, on the other hand, used a bewildering range of other techniques: glazed bricks, carved and glazed terracotta, tile mosaic and *cuerda seca*, overglaze enamelling, underglaze painted relief tiles and occasionally lustre.

Particularly striking in the Timurid period is not only that tiles seem to cover every available surface – Robert Hillenbrand has appropriately described this as a 'veil of tilework increasingly unconnected with the structural forms beneath' – but that in the same building two or three techniques may be used for different areas. Large wall surfaces are often decorated with glazed bricks, for instance, while areas such as panels over doorways are in tile mosaic.

Long before the Islamic period, glazed coloured bricks had decorated brick buildings in Iran and Mesopotamia. In the Islamic period, Arab chroniclers from the tenth century onwards talk of blue coloured domes in the mosques and palaces of this region. The thirteenth-century geographer Yaqut described the tomb of the Seljuq Sultan Sanjar at Merv, erected in about 1152, where the blue dome could be seen while still a day's journey away. The use of glazed tiles to decorate Timurid monuments completely is, however, simply the logical outcome of the gradual introduction into brick architecture of a variety of elements, initially unglazed, placed so as to interrupt the brick surfaces. On early medieval buildings particular areas, such as inscriptions, began to be high-lighted with blue tiles: an early example is the minaret of the Masjid-i Jamiʿ at Damghan (c.1058). Blue glazed plugs between the plain bricks were another way of visually breaking up the façade.

The gradual increased use of these glazed elements has been documented by Donald Wilber on a series of buildings over a two-hundred-year period, culminating in the mausoleum of the Il-Khanid Sultan Uljaitu (begun in 1310):

> With the mausoleum of Olcaitu [*sic*] the technique of mosaic faience had arrived at maturity. Associated with the new mastery of the medium came full awareness of its possibilities – that mosaic faience could be used in an unlimited variety of patterns, on surfaces of any shape and contour, and on interiors equally well as on exteriors.

Thus the stage was set. At Sultaniyah are examples of the *banna'i* technique, used extensively under the Timurids: a particularly effective development in which the glazed bricks laid on their ends form zigzag patterns or monumental inscriptions. The bold designs in cobalt blue and turquoise contrast dramatically with the honey-coloured background of the brick façades. The *banna'i* technique is used with striking effect, for instance, on the great tower-like bastions of the late fourteenth-century Aq Saray and, within its massive portal, above the panels of *cuerda seca* and tile mosaic. Ulugh Beg, Timur's grandson, was also fond of the *banna'i* tech-nique, and on his buildings, particularly his *madrasah* (built 1417–21) on the Registan Square at Samarqand, square Kufic inscriptions spelling out the words Allah, Muhammad and ʿAli boldly adorn the exterior walls.

Also at Sultaniyah are found some of the earliest examples in Iran of what Wilber describes as 'complete' tile mosaic (as op-posed to individual elements of glazing). Contrasting with the spare and elegant use of colour achieved with glazed bricks, by the Timurid period the designs in tile mosaic have become dense and exuberant. Adopted first in Anatolia for internal use at the begin-ning of the thirteenth century and by the Muzaffarids in south-western Iran in the mid fourteenth century, extensive early use of tile mosaic in Timurid architecture can be seen at the Aq Saray: geometric panels and inscriptions and complex floral designs within vases in designs which are quite different in character to the

59 ABOVE AND OPPOSITE, ABOVE Narrow border tiles, stone-paste, decorated in *cuerda seca* and gilded, late 14th–15th century. Similar tiles are found in the Bibi Khanum in Samarqand (1398–1405) and in the Madrasat al-Ghiyathiyah at Khargird (1442–6). Average dimensions: 30.5×11 cm.

60 RIGHT 15th-century tile mosaic panel in the Great Mosque in Zabid in Yemen. It is not clear how this arrived in Yemen, a country with no tradition of tilework. It may have been brought as a gift by one of the Iranian *'ulama* who were frequent visitors to Yemen in medieval times. It was probably installed in the mosque during renovations that took place in 1492.

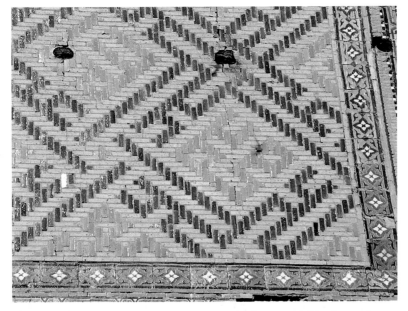

61 LEFT Detail of *banna'i* technique in the Aq Sarai palace at Shahr-i Sabz (1379–96). The glazed bricks form the words Allah, Muhammad and 'Ali.

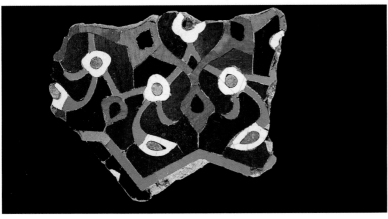

62 LEFT Fragmentary stone-paste tile mosaic star tile, early 15th century, part of a group collected by the Hon. Colonel E. Yate from the minarets of the Musalla of Gauhar Shad in Herat after they had been pulled down in 1885. 15×18 cm.

cuerda seca tile panels lying alongside them. Tile mosaic is used exclusively in another early example, the tomb of Timur's sister Shirin Biqa (built 1385–6) in the Shah-i Zindah in Samarqand, in a style that Lisa Golombek has attributed to Iranian artists. The full range and development of tile mosaic can be seen on a number of important monuments of the fifteenth century, for instance the mosque of Gauhar Shad in Herat (1417–38), the Ulugh Beg *madrasah* in Samarqand (1417–20) and the *madrasah* in Khargird (1444). On the Blue Mosque in Tabriz, capital of the Qaraqoyunlu dynasty built between 1462 and 1465, there are magnificent floral repeat patterns of lotus flowers picked out in white with turquoise stems against the cobalt blue ground. Tile mosaic was not restricted to the buildings alone but was also used on a series of *minbars* in mosques in central Iran dating between 1445 and 1535. The finest example of these is in the Masjid-i Maydan at Kashan, signed by a craftsman who called himself 'Haydar the tile cutter' (*kashi tarash*).

Tile mosaic was an extremely time-consuming technique, yet once it had taken root and there were sufficient craftsmen proficient in it, it was practised right up until the nineteenth century in Central Asia, and in Iran under the Safavids. Even today in Iran, Central Asia and Afghanistan craftsmen continue to use the technique for restoring tiles on historic monuments.

Side by side with tile mosaic we also find tiles decorated in *cuerda seca*, a technique developed in Central Asia in the second half of the fourteenth century. Some of the earliest examples, from about the 1370s, are found in the Shah-i Zindah in Samarqand and in the Aq Saray at Shahr-i Sabz. Typical *cuerda seca* tiles of the late fourteenth and early fifteenth century are decorated with arabesque and floral motifs, often contained in cartouches which sometimes have yellow outlines. Complex star patterns also appear, as do inscriptions in an elaborate Kufic script, often outlined in black and sometimes in gold. In general, the predominant background colour is blue, but other colours have been used including apple green, white, yellow, black and red in addition to the gold, which at Aq Saray is still as brilliant as when Clavijo saw it. The shapes of tiles decorated in *cuerda seca* vary greatly: there are single stars or pentagons set into the brick façades; rectangular concave tiles are used on columns; and square or hexagonal tiles make up large panels.

The techniques discussed so far – glazed bricks (*banna'i*), tile mosaic and *cuerda seca* – are all found in the Shah-i Zindah. This extraordinary necropolis consisting largely of single-chamber tombs is built on a narrow street on the mound of Afrasiyab to the

63 *Cuerda seca* star tile, stone-paste, mid 15th century. This is one of a number in Western collections from the Madrasat al-Ghiyathiyah at Khargird (1442–6). The building was constructed for Ghiyath al-Din Pir Ahmad Khvafi, one of the viziers of Timur's son Shah Rukh. Maximum DIAM: 39.5 cm.

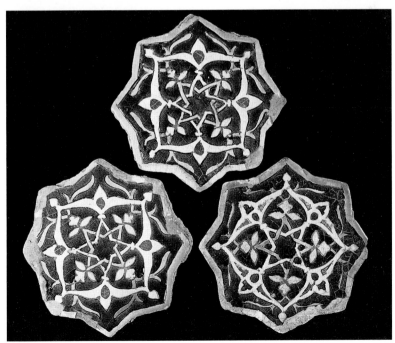

64 *Cuerda seca* star tiles, stone-paste, mid 15th century. Tiles such as these would have been inset into brick façades. The arabesques and flowers are reserved against a deep cobalt ground. The borders are turquoise. Average DIAM: 22 cm.

65 *Cuerda seca* tile, stone-paste, 15th century. The square Kufic inscription is outlined in red and filled with gold. The bubbly surface of the glaze indicates that it has 'crawled' during firing. It is said to have come from the tomb of Sheikh Baha al-Din Nuri at Khojand in Turkestan. Maximum W: 30 cm.

66 RIGHT *Cuerda seca* convex tile, stone-paste, 15th century. Such tiles were used on columns on a number of Timurid monuments. This example closely resembles column tiles in the Bibi Khanum in Samarqand (begun 1398). The red outlines are filled with gold and a delicate apple green is applied to the cartouches. 12×16 cm.

67 OPPOSITE Detail of the façade of the mausoleum of Shad-i Mulk Aga (*c.*1371–83) in the Shah-i Zindah, Samarqand. The façade is decorated with carved and glazed terracotta. A round *lajvardina* tile is in the centre of the polylobed medallion.

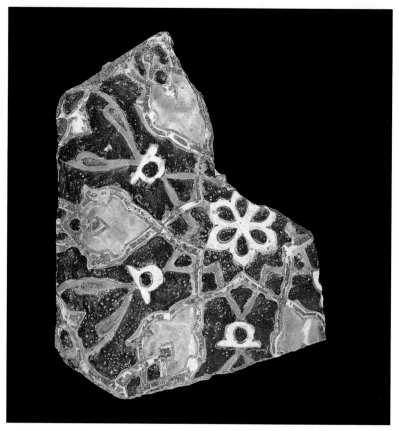

north of Samarqand. Its foundation was associated with a cult figure called Qusam b. ʿAbbas, and the earliest monuments date back to the eleventh century. What is of interest in the present context is a series of tombs, densely decorated inside and out, built between about 1370 and 1405 for the Timurid aristocracy, many of them women. One of the predominant techniques is carved and glazed terracotta, the finest example being the tomb of Shad-i 67 Mulk Aga (1371–83). The thick panels are deeply cut with inscriptions and foliate designs within a strict geometric framework. The principal colour is a rich turquoise blue, with darker blue backgrounds and white outlines. This highly attractive technique predates the Timurid conquest – one of the earliest examples is a fragment in the Victoria and Albert Museum dated AH 722/AD 1322, said to come from 'a mosque in the Shah-i Zindah' – and seems only to have been used during the fourteenth century. A splendid early example is the tomb of Buyan Quli Khan (d. 1358) in Bukhara, which was once totally revetted in tiles of this technique, inside and out. Little now survives, though there are several panels and a pilaster from the tomb in the Victoria and Albert Museum. Not simply confined to wall decoration, the technique is also found on a late fourteenth-century cenotaph at Fusanj near Herat, the only example known outside Central Asia.

Another legacy from the pre-Timurid period are two other

68 14th-century *lajvardina* tile, stone-paste, painted in yellow, red and white over a cobalt ground. The moulded inscription 'Ay Muharram' presumably refers to the month of Muharram, which is the first in the Muslim year and associated particularly with Shiite festivals. 16.5×25.5 cm.

techniques used in a more limited way on the Shah-i Zindah tombs: overglaze enamelled *lajvardina* and underglaze painted tiles. The *lajvardina* tiles with their characteristic cobalt ground are in a variety of shapes, painted over the glaze in white and red, and appear in a number of the tombs. The finest examples are in that of Ulugh Sultan Begum (c.1385). The underglaze painted tiles are equally interesting; the most accomplished of these are in the tomb of Shad-i Mulk Aga (d. 1385). The chinoiserie lotus flowers painted white in relief against the blue ground are reminiscent of the Sultanabad style of Il-Khanid Iran a century earlier.

Similar underglaze-painted relief tiles are also found in Khiva, on the mid fourteenth-century cenotaph of Sayyid ʿAla al-Din, and Michael Rogers has argued that it is tiles such as these that are likely to have provided inspiration for the underglaze-painted tiles that adorn the magnificent eighteenth and nineteenth-century revivalist architecture in the city built when it was capital of the Uzbeg Khanate (1780–1850). Vast *madrasahs*, mosques, mausolea and a citadel were constructed within the confines of a city wall, much of which survives. Such was the speed of construction that many of the tiles appear to have been nailed on, numbers clearly painted on the surface as a guide for the installation.

SAFAVIDS

After Timur's death in 1405, his territories were divided among his sons and grandsons. While his concerns had been principally military, his successors, Shah Rukh, Ulugh Beg, Abu Saʿid and Husayn Bayqara, were able to spend more time on the arts. They continued the precedent set by Timur, commissioning monumental architecture in the main Timurid cities where they presided over courts whose artistic achievements were outstanding, particularly in the realm of book production.

The end of the Timurid era came in the early part of the sixteenth century. Their territories to the east were conquered by the Uzbeg Shaybanids, who took Herat in 1507, while in the west Ismaʿil, with the support of Turkish tribesmen known as Qizil Bash (red heads, after their red caps), became the first ruler of the great Shiite dynasty of the Safavids (1501–1732), whose eponymous founder Shaykh Safi al-Din (d. 1334) was buried at Ardabil.

Of the wide variety of techniques used for decorating tilework in the Timurid period, tile mosaic and *cuerda seca* were most extensively used in Safavid Iran, with some decorated in underglaze. The principal elements of design and the Timurid aesthetic of overall tiling continued without a break. Early examples are tile

69 Underglaze painted relief tiles with chinoiserie lotus flowers around the central medallion. In situ, tomb of Shad-i Mulk Aga (*c.*1371–83) in the Shah-i Zindah, Samarqand.

70 BELOW 18th–19th-century underglaze painted tiles at Khiva. Nails were frequently used to hold the tiles in place.

mosaic revetments in the mausoleum of Harun Vilayat, built in 1512 in Isfahan, while the most magnificent tilework was produced in the later part of the century during the reign of Shah ʿAbbas I (1588–1629). His great vision was the city of Isfahan to where he transferred his capital, previously at Qazvin, in 1599. 'Isfahan could not have been conceived and executed except by kings and architects who spent their days and nights listening to the Thousand and One Nights', wrote Gobineau. The focus of the city was the Maydan-i Shah, a vast central area which also served as a polo ground, around which he built a series of mosques, a bazaar and palaces. Like Timur he loved gardens; Tavernier, writing in 1633, marvelled that from 'whatever side one arrives . . . one discovers first of all the minarets of the mosques, then trees surrounding the houses, so that from afar Isfahan resembles more a forest than a city'.

Cuerda seca and tile mosaic

Safavid mosques and *madrasahs* are totally clad in a mantle of tiles inside and out, the use of tiles even more extensive than under the Timurids. What distinguishes Safavid from Timurid religious monuments is the uniformity of the tilework. The vast expanses tend to be covered by variations of one pattern: endlessly repeating and extending floral motifs. Safavid tiles can be divided into

71 Early 20th-century colour-tinted lantern slide by Reginald A. Malby FRPS, of the Maydan-i Shah in Isfahan showing the Masjid-i Shah built in 1612–37. Malby, who died in 1924, was much admired for his technical expertise and gave popular lantern slide lectures.

several stylistic groups, the designs largely reflecting the function of the buildings they adorn – religious edifices, palaces, and an idiosyncratic mixture of styles in New Julfa, the Armenian suburb of Isfahan.

While tile mosaic continued to be employed, Shah ʿAbbas' impatience to see his religious monuments completed encouraged greater use of the speedier *cuerda seca* technique. The Masjid-i Shaykh Lutfallah (1602) on the east side of the Maydan-i Shah has both tile mosaic and *cuerda seca* for different sections of the building and different types of decoration within it. The inscriptions are in tile mosaic, as are some of the large floral designs, with elaborate cartouches, while the dado panels are painted in *cuerda seca* and look like carpets. This is no accident. As under the Timurids, there was a well-defined court style and it is therefore not surprising to see the same elements repeated in carpets, textiles, and book bindings and illumination. The motifs, based on the Timurid repertoire, are principally floral patterns, with dense designs of flowers such as chrysanthemums or chinoiserie lotuses on winding scrolls with feathery leaves. Inscriptions are usually in *nastaʿliq* script with the occasional use of Kufic as in the dome of Masjid-i Shaykh Lutfallah. Blue is the predominant colour but in the Masjid-i Shah, on the south side of the Maydan-i Shah (begun *c.*1611), the blue is contrasted with a brilliant chrome yellow. The last of the great Safavid religious monuments of Isfahan is the Madrasah Madar-i Shah (1706–14), built by Shah Sultan Husayn (1694–1722).

In the palaces of Isfahan, *cuerda seca* tiles constitute another of the stylistic groups of Safavid tiles. These tiles generally form pictures, each tile painted with one element of an overall scene. 72– The most complete cycle in situ, probably among the latest of the surviving tiles, is in the Hasht Behesht (the Palace of the Eight Paradises) in the Garden of the Nightingales. Panels from it are now in various museums including the Los Angeles County Museum. Built in 1669 by Shah Sulayman (1666–94), the panels contain extraordinary representations of mythical beasts, genii and scenes of animal fights derived from ancient Iran. Resembling large-scale versions of miniature paintings on paper, with striking similarities particularly in the depictions of costume, the tile pictures may have been based on designs provided by court painters.

The numerous pictorial tiles now scattered among Museum collections suggest that many of the pavilions which so impressed Western travellers were adorned with such tiles and not only painted in *cuerda seca* but also in the underglaze Kubachi style (see

page 79). Friedrich Sarre, travelling in Iran in the early part of this century, saw tile panels in various locations including a palace (now destroyed) at the north end of the Chahar Bagh in Isfahan. *Cuerda seca* panels now in the Metropolitan Museum of Art and the Louvre are likely to have come from this palace. The subject matter of these tile panels with their scenes of hunting and feasting is similar to that of the murals which also adorned the palaces. In the absence of any contemporary descriptions of tiles, Pietro della Valle's account of murals in a palace in Isfahan (probably the 'Ali Qapu, built in 1598) is worth quoting:

The king's Casino or summer house has on the walls of the apartments here and there various recessed panels in which there are all kinds of painted figures; but since they do not as we do follow the practise of painting historical or mythological scenes, all these figures simply show men and women either alone or in groups in lascivious postures. Some stand with cups and flagons of wine in their hands drinking; some are in drunken sleep; others are growing tipsy and about to fall down; and there are various other postures on show, all representing Venus and Bacchus combined. Among these figures, which are almost all in the costume of the country, are also many painted wearing hats, by which they mean without any other indication from the clothing Western Christians.

Under the Safavids there was a vogue for portraying the numerous foreigners who visited the court, whether in murals as della Valle describes, in miniatures or in tilework, as seen in the British Museum tile arch.

A third stylistic group of Safavid tiles is to be found in New Julfa, the Armenian suburb of Isfahan. Shah 'Abbas had moved

72 Detail from *cuerda seca* architectural spandrel, stone-paste, depicting an outdoor scene replicated on both sides. The wide-brimmed hats on some of the figures denote that these are probably Europeans. 17th century, with some sections possibly 19th century.
350.5×167.7 cm.

the community in 1604 from old Julfa in Azerbaijan to his capital, needing them for their skills and trading contacts. New Julfa was marvelled at by the Europeans who visited it; Sir John Chardin, writing in 1666, says there were over 3400 houses, 'some so richly gilded that one would call them palaces'. Many houses and churches were painted with murals which the Muslims wondered at (Pietro della Valle thought them appallingly bad). The churches, of which thirteen survive, were mostly built in the first half of the seventeenth century, and in a number of them there are remarkable *cuerda seca* tile panels. The designs are a fascinating mixture of traditional floral designs with occasional figures, and in All Saviour's Cathedral (built 1658–72) there are bands of angels. Although similar to the Persian *cuerda seca* tiles in Isfahan, their subject matter and the presence of Armenian inscriptions would imply that they were made by Armenian craftsmen.

73 OPPOSITE *Cuerda seca* stone-paste tile from a panel of picture tiles probably from a palace, first half of 17th century. The archer's pose and costume are comparable to contemporary Persian miniatures.
HT: 16.5 cm.

Underglaze painted tiles

Underglaze painted tiles were produced in much smaller quantities during the Safavid period and their place of manufacture is unknown. Still in situ are tiles in the bath of Ganje ʿAli Khan in Kirman, painted in blue and red and possibly made in the town of Kirman itself, which was known as a centre for the production of pottery vessels. A large tile in the British Museum painted in blue and black in the shape of a *mihrab* may also belong to this group.

Kubachi ware is the name given to a particular group of underglaze painted pottery that includes a large number of vessels and some tiles, probably destined for palaces (see page 76), that are thought to have been produced in north-western Iran, probably in the vicinity of Tabriz, between the fifteenth and seventeenth centuries. The name comes from finds of this pottery in the village of Kubacha in Daghestan in the Caucasus by a Russian scholar at the end of the nineteenth century, and many of the best examples are in the Hermitage in St Petersburg. There are several groups of Kubachi ware, including vessels with decoration largely derived from blue-and-white Chinese porcelain of the fourteenth to fifteenth century and a rare group painted in black under a green glaze. Another group of Kubachi ware (which includes tiles) shows the influence of the Iznik colour scheme of the mid sixteenth century, with polychrome colours painted under the glaze. Two examples in the Victoria and Albert Museum are believed to have come from a palace in the eastern Iranian province of Khurasan. Pieces in this group frequently contain figural designs, often languid figures akin to those in contemporary Persian miniatures. The rare surviving tiles are often painted with scantily dressed

74

75

dancing girls reminiscent of Pietro della Valle's mural descriptions (see page 77). The style of drawing is looser and less stylised than that of the figures painted in the *cuerda seca* tile pictures. One of the British Museum examples has a realistic picture of a woman carrying a baby.

ZAND AND QAJAR PERIODS

In the eighteenth century, Iran was in chaos following the Afghan invasions and the demise of the Safavids in 1732. It was not until the reign of Karim Khan Zand (1750–79) that building resumed on an ambitious scale, particularly in his capital at Shiraz. With it came a new impetus for the tile industry. Tile pictures were produced in the Safavid tradition, with the introduction of a new colour, pink, which was also used in the succeeding Qajar period (1783–1924). In the Qajar capital at Tehran two rulers, Fath ʿAli Shah (1797–1839) and Nasir al-Din Shah (1848–96), built a series of monuments, largely tiled, which provide a group of dated material for the study of Qajar tilework. The techniques included both *cuerda seca* and underglaze, sometimes combined with moulded designs. The themes in the Gulistan and Sultanabad palaces in Tehran include views of buildings and images of Nasir al-Din Shah reviewing his troops. There were also scenes from Persian folk history.

78   Single tiles in museum collections or placed around fireplaces in English country houses were brought back by visitors to Iran and represent a nineteenth-century continuation of Safavid themes such as figures in landscapes, often out riding. These tiles, produced in the second half of the nineteenth century, are distinguished by a delicate rendering of colour. An interesting tile in the 77 British Museum shows a new preoccupation, the depiction of scenes from Iran's pre-Islamic past. Inspired by excavations at Persepolis ordered by the governor of Fars in the 1870s, a vogue for imitation Achaemenid sculptures became popular among the urban élite of Shiraz. Judith Lerner has pointed out that the scene on the British Museum tile is virtually identical to that on an alabaster panel, modelled on a Persepolis bas relief, set above the fireplace in a house known as the Narangistan, completed in 1885. It is thought that the craftsmen and artists in Shiraz would have copied from popular guides to the antiquities produced during this period. It may be that such tiles were also produced in Shiraz, although it has traditionally been thought that Tehran and Isfahan were the main centres.

    A number of Qajar potters and tilemakers signed their works; 79 one such is Muhammad Ibrahim, whose signature appears on a

74 OPPOSITE Large tile, stone-paste, possibly from a cenotaph, 17th–18th(?) century. Painted in blue and black on a white ground, in the centre is a *mihrab* arch with a hanging lamp. Around the sides are inscriptions from the Qur'an, *surah* 11, part of v. 255, and the names of some of the imams revered by Shiite Muslims. In the lower register is the phrase 'There is no God but Allah, Muhammad is the Prophet and Ali is in truth the friend of God', and above it is a verse of Persian poetry: 'Reflect by the graveside after death and observe how from the flames of my heart smoke emerges from the shroud' (after Hafiz). 69×41 cm.

75 A panel of three underglaze-painted stone-paste 'Kubachi' tiles, 16th century. They are painted in polychrome colours under the glaze with figures in a variety of poses including a woman carrying a baby. Such tiles were made for the palaces or pavilions that were built by the Safavid rulers throughout Iran. 26.5×46 cm.

tile in the British Museum. The best-known Qajar potter was 'Ali Muhammad Isfahani, who wrote a treatise on ceramic production (and whose work has been published by Jennifer Scarce). About twenty known pieces of tilework are attributed to him. He was patronised by Major-General Sir Robert Murdoch Smith, who was in Iran between 1865 and 1888 working as Director of the Persian Telegraph Department and was also collecting in particular for the South Kensington (later Victoria and Albert) Museum. His interest was the preservation of the old crafts, especially ceramics. In 1884 he wrote to the Museum:

I have ordered some wall tiles to be made at Isfahan by a clever young potter there, who for the last few years has been making experiments in imitation of the tiles in the old Safavean buildings in that city. Some specimens of his last productions which I saw recently struck me as highly artistic, the designs so original, only the paste, the glaze and the general style of the old examples being imitated.

76 Square tile, stone-paste, painted in a range
of underglaze colours including blue, pink and
yellow on a white ground, 19th century.
Depicted are a mulla and two onlookers. It was
acquired in Kerbela. 20.5×20.5 cm.

77 Rectangular tile, stone-paste, with moulded decoration painted under the glaze in delicate polychrome colours including pink against a dark blue ground. Third quarter of the 19th century. Depicted is an Achaemenid ruler with his attendant holding a flywhisk behind him, and three soldiers. Under the ruler's throne are the words 'King Jamshid'. Shiraz or Tehran. 30×31 cm.

78 Rectangular tile, stone-paste with moulded decoration painted under the glaze. Third quarter of the 19th century. Three figures in a landscape, the one on the left with his foppish turban possibly representing a foreigner, the woman playing a lute. Above the horseman is the mythical bird Huma, whose shadow was cast only over princely persons. Shiraz or Tehran. 30×31 cm.

INDIA

Demonstrating the far-reaching effect of Iranian and Central Asian traditions of tilework are Indian tiles, of which the British Museum has only a few examples; a far more extensive collection is in the Victoria and Albert Museum. Although there is some evidence for the use of tiles in India during the early centuries of this era, tiles were not extensively employed until after the introduction of Islam in medieval times. The same dichotomy appears to exist in the use of tilework in India as in the eastern and western Islamic lands, where tiles were most often used on brick rather than stone architecture except in the Mughal period, when they were used on both. The predominant use of tiles was on brick façades in Bengal, Sindh and Multan, while in the Deccan tiles are combined sparsely with stone façades or appear on buildings which, uncharacteristically for the area, were built of brick.

Bengal

The fragments of Bengal tiles in the collection were picked up in Gaur, site of one of the capitals of the Bengal sultanate (1204–1576). This long, narrow, now ruined city on a branch of the river Ganges in eastern India was filled with beautiful mosques and tombs built of brick with partial black stone facing. Tilework was used sparsely. One of the earliest buildings with tiles in Bengal is the Ekhlati mosque at nearby Pandua (c.1431). The surviving Gaur tiles in the British Museum (the building they came from is unknown) are in a variety of shapes, and glazed in either black or 80 white, with slip painting; one of these is painted in *cuerda seca*. Both the technique and the design of this tile undoubtedly originated in Iran. The central lotus flower and split leaf palmettes are an example of the international Timurid style and show how extraordinarily far-reaching and influential this style was.

The Deccan and Multan

A group of hexagonal and rectangular tiles in the British Museum 82 come from Bijapur, the capital of one of the Deccani sultanates (c.1500–1686). The design of these tiles again exhibits the strong influence of the Timurid style, while the blue-and-white colour scheme links them to the fifteenth-century chinoiserie tiles of Syria. Contemporary tiles found in Goa also show the same connections. The presence of numerous Iranians in the Deccan – sheikhs and merchants as well as workmen – is demonstrated by the Persian appearance of the *madrasah* of Mahmud Gawan at Bidar, built in 1472, with its *banna'i* and tile mosaic façade.

The blue-and-white colour scheme combined with turquoise 81 links the tiles of Bijapur to the extensive tilework of Sindh and Multan – like the Deccan, areas that had strong trading connections with the central Islamic lands. Some of the finest examples are on the fourteenth-century tomb of Rukn-i Alam at Multan. Tiles are still produced in Multan today using the same colour scheme, and with an identical rich red earthenware body, modern tiles are difficult to distinguish from the old.

Mughal tiles

83 Used on both stone and brick surfaces, Mughal tiles show a strong Safavid influence in style and technique, as do many of the other arts of the period. The single Mughal *cuerda seca* tile in the British

79 OPPOSITE Square tile, stone-paste, painted in polychrome underglaze colours with a scene from the *Shahnameh*, a polo match between Siyavush and Afrasiyab, to whose court Siyavush had fled after quarrelling with his father, the king of Iran. The scene is described in the Persian inscription around the sides. The cartouches at the top contain the signature of the potter Muhammad Ibrahim, whose work is also known from pottery vessels. 30×30 cm.

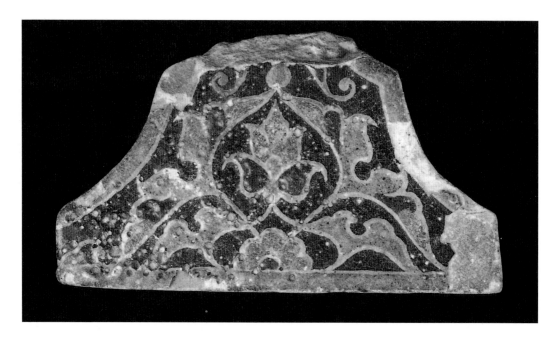

80 *Cuerda seca* earthenware tile, painted in yellow and green on a black ground, part of a group of 15th-century tiles from Gaur in Bengal. 7×13.5 cm.

Museum has a characteristic brilliant yellow ground with red flowers outlined in white and with a green leaf that bears some resemblance to the Ottoman *saz* leaf, showing the typical diversity of sources – both Indian and foreign – that make up Mughal art.

In the next chapter we turn westwards to Egypt, Syria and Turkey where a number of themes will be explored: the export to the west of Timurid techniques and decorative styles, further inspiration from China and the full blossoming of underglaze painting, leading to the development of the most magnificent tiles of all – those from the potteries at Iznik. What is dramatically different in this next phase is the approach to tilework. While in Iran and Central Asia the tiles seem to form a natural part of the brick architecture they adorned, in the western Islamic lands tiles were generally affixed to stone façades to very different effect.

81 Rectangular earthenware inscriptional tile
painted in underglaze blue and turquoise on a
white ground. Multan, c.16th century.
Maximum dimension: 19.5 cm.

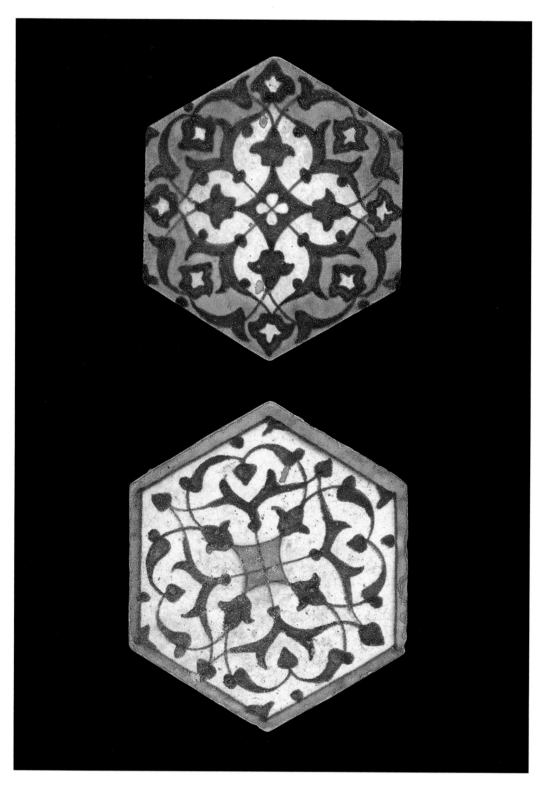

82 OPPOSITE Hexagonal *c.*16th-century underglaze-painted earthenware tiles from Bijapur, painted in underglaze cobalt and turquoise. The designs form part of the repertoire of the international Timurid style. Average DIAM: 16.5 cm.

83 ABOVE Square *cuerda seca* earthenware tile, part of a panel, painted in brilliant yellow, red, green and brown. Mughal, 17th century. 19.5×19.5 cm.

— 5 —

Lotus Flowers
and Tulips
Syria and Turkey
15th–19th Centuries

In this chapter we shall consider three main groups of tiles. The first are chinoiserie underglaze-painted tiles of the fifteenth century; the second are tiles made in Turkey in the Timurid traditions of tile mosaic and *cuerda seca*; and the third are the magnificent polychrome tiles associated with the kilns of Iznik. The two dynasties whose rule dominates the period under discussion are the Mamluks (1250–1517) in Egypt and Syria and the Ottomans (1281–1924), whose empire at its height absorbed the Mamluk domains and reached far into North Africa and Europe.

The Sunni dynasty of the Mamluks took over power from the Ayyubids in Egypt and Syria in 1250. Originally slaves imported from Central Asia and the Caucasus, the Mamluks (their name means slave) became a powerful military force in the region. They put an end to the Mongol threat to their kingdom at the battle of 'Ayn Jalut in 1260 and by the end of the same century had expelled the Crusaders. Their wealth, acquired largely as a result of their involvement in the Indian Ocean trade, enabled them to be lavish patrons. All spheres of art benefited: extraordinary and ostentatious Mamluk monuments still dominate the Cairo skyline and beautifully illuminated manuscripts, fine metalwork and ceramics were produced which survive in large quantities.

Cairo and Damascus were the chief centres of the ceramic industry which produced wares in a variety of techniques and styles. The importance of Damascus can be gauged from signatures on pots; a famous example is the lustre jar in the Al-Sabah collection on which is inscribed that it was made by Yusuf in Damascus. Further evidence comes from Venetian records requesting '*alberegli Domaschini*', as well as numerous sherds, including tile fragments, found in the Bab al-Sharqi quarter of the city. That Cairo was equally important has been revealed by excavations in the potters' quarter at Fustat, old Cairo. Largely associated with Damascus were the lustre albarellos or drug jars, decorated with golden lustre over a cobalt ground. Earthenware slip-painted pottery, often bearing Mamluk heraldic blazons, was made in Cairo, and Cairene potters also produced plausible imitations of Chinese celadon. Underglaze blue-and-white painted vessels and tiles were made at both centres.

As suggested earlier, tilework was a more natural adjunct to brick rather than stone architecture. Tiling was nonetheless used on stone architecture in Anatolia in the thirteenth and fourteenth centuries – significantly, often in sections of brickwork. In Syria and in Egypt, with their largely stone buildings, there are some scattered examples of tilework from the thirteenth and fourteenth centuries. However, it was not until the fifteenth century that the possibilities of using tiles were fully explored in this region.

CHINESE BLUE-AND-WHITE

Imported Chinese porcelain of the Tang and Song periods had already made an impact on the Islamic ceramics industry in preceding centuries under the ʿAbbasids in Iraq in the ninth and tenth centuries and during the Seljuq and Il-Khanid periods in Iran between the twelfth and fourteenth centuries. Now it was Yuan and Ming blue-and-white that was to revolutionise the designs and colour scheme of Mamluk pottery. These porcelains were highly regarded by monarchs and wealthy alike in the Near East, and there are superb collections in the Topkapi palace in Istanbul and from the Ardabil Shrine in Iran. It was imported by sea through the main ports, one of them being Aden. The fourteenth-century Rasulid Sultan al-Malik al-Ashraf (1377–1401) proudly displayed 'five hundred dishes of Chinese porcelain that had never been used' on the occasion of his son's circumcision feast. Chinese porcelain has been found at various Near Eastern sites including Hormuz on the Persian Gulf, Fustat (old Cairo) and Hama in central Syria. Several hundred pieces, carefully treasured and handed down from generation to generation, came to light in

84 Chinese porcelain floor tiles painted in underglaze cobalt blue with a rosette and foliate motifs. Ming dynasty, mid 15th century. 23×23 cm.

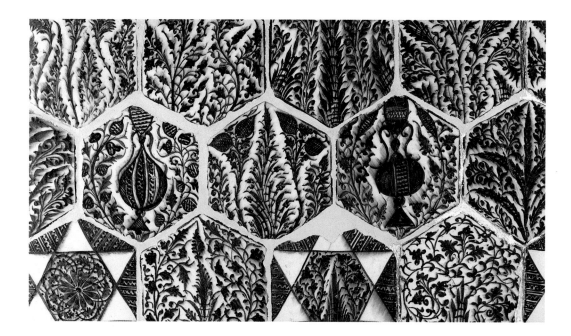

Douma near Damascus during the course of demolition of houses in the 1960s.

While it is generally known that Chinese blue-and-white vessels were exported to the Near East in large quantities, an intriguing reference in the memoirs of the Mughal emperor Babur (d. 1526) and the recent acquisition of two fifteenth-century Ming floor tiles by the British Museum suggest that limited numbers of Chinese tiles, too, may have been made for the Near Eastern market during this time. Babur mentions that Timur's grandson Ulugh Beg had a *chini-khaneh* of which the walls were apparently faced with porcelain tiles brought over from China. Chinese blue-and-white tiles are known in the Near East and India from a later period and have been documented by John Carswell. These include seventeenth to eighteenth-century examples in the Armenian Cathedral of St James in Jerusalem, the Beylerbey mosque in Istanbul and a magnificent series of landscape tiles in the synagogue in Cochin in southern India. The designs of the unique fifteenth-century Ming tiles in the British Museum with their arabesque motifs certainly suggest that these were made with a Near Eastern market in mind, but as they appeared on the art market with no details of provenance we cannot be certain where they were destined.

The Islamic imitations of Chinese blue-and-white are fascinating. While vessels produced in Syria in the late fourteenth century are in a style remarkably similar to the Chinese originals, by the middle of the fifteenth century the Chinese motifs had been

85 Panel of hexagonal tiles, stone-paste, painted in underglaze blue. Egypt or Syria, first half of 15th century. The designs combine Chinese-inspired foliate with more Islamic motifs, such as the geometric designs of the lower tiles and the bulbous ewers. Average DIAM: 18 cm.

84

95

absorbed and transformed and a delightful hybrid Chinese–
Islamic style had emerged. There are several groups of fifteenth-
century underglaze-painted tiles decorated in this hybrid style.
Although not all produced by the same workshops, they can be
discussed together because of their general similarity of style and
the common source of their decorative designs.

The main groups of blue-and-white tiles still in situ are in the
mosque and tomb of the Mamluk dignitary Ghars al-Din Khalil
al-Tawrizi in Damascus (c.1420), and in the mosque of Murad II
in Edirne (1435–6) in north-western Turkey. Odd groups survive
in Egypt (now in the Museum of Islamic Art), elsewhere in
Turkey, in Syria and Lebanon and in a number of museum collections, in particular the Victoria and Albert Museum, with a small
group acquired by the British Museum in the 1980s. The tiles are
predominantly hexagonal, painted on a white ground in cobalt or
occasionally in black under a transparent glaze and sometimes
with turquoise or blue borders. They are set either on their points
or on their sides and are sometimes interspersed with plain trian-
gular turquoise tiles. Their decorative motifs consist of gently
swaying, feathery trees, bulbous-bodied ewers or star-shaped
designs, while others are decorated with more loosely vegetal
ornament or birds.

The overall technical and stylistic similarities between the various surviving groups of blue-and-white tiles – although there are
perceptible differences in the drawing style – have indeed
suggested the possible existence of a group of itinerant potters
setting up temporary workshops or working in existing workshops in a variety of centres. What at least two of the groups have
in common, apart from their stylistic similarity, is a connection
with Tabriz. On one of the panels in the Tawrizi mosque in
Damascus is the Arabic inscription ʿamal Ghaibi al-Tawrizi (the
work of Ghaibi al-Tawrizi). The name, referring either to a person
or a workshop, occurs on the base of numerous c. fifteenth-
century blue-and-white sherds form Fustat. A further connection
with Tabriz is in the name of the Mamluk official who commissioned the mosque, who has the nisbah al-Tawrizi. Others potters
who sign themselves 'the masters of Tabriz' in the Green Mosque
in Bursa (1419–29) are also associated with the production of the
other main group of fifteenth-century blue-and-white tiles at the
mosque of Murad II at Erdirne. These potters were responsible for
tilework in a series of mosques and tombs in Turkey, using techniques of underglaze, tile mosaic (in the Iranian rather than
Anatolian style) and cuerda seca (introduced to Turkey for the
first time). It is their work that we shall next consider.

85–8

86 Hexagonal tile, stone-paste, painted in underglaze black and blue with a turquoise border. Egypt or Syria, first half of 15th century. The central design is of a bulbous Islamic ewer. 19×17.5 cm.

87 Square tile, stone-paste, painted in underglaze black and blue with arabesque ornament. Egypt or Syria, first half of 15th century. 23.4×23 cm.

IRANIAN POTTERS IN TURKEY

The fall of the Seljuqs of Rum in 1307 brought to an end the glorious phase of architecture in Anatolia and its magnificent tilework (see page 58). The last major Anatolian building with tilework is the complex at Beyşehir (1296–1301). It is not until the beginning of the fifteenth century in Bursa that we find any tiles of note in Turkey and these exhibit, both technically and stylistically, a strong influence from Iran and Central Asia.

This Timurid influence on Turkish tilework came about in a number of ways. After the defeat of the Ottomans at the battle of Ankara in 1402, Timur carried craftsmen off to his capital at Samarqand. Among these was the designer Nakkaş 'Ali who, on his return to his homeland, supervised the mosque and tomb complex of Mehmed I in Bursa (built between 1419 and 1424) also known as the Green Mosque and Tomb. The style that such artists brought back to Turkey from Iran and Central Asia is known as the international Timurid style (see page 64). Its characteristics – organic floral and foliate designs that are an extraordinary synthesis of traditional 'Islamic' motifs such as the arabesque with Chinese-inspired designs – found their way not only into tilework but into other forms of Ottoman art of the fifteenth century such as bookbindings and album drawings.

The complex of Mehmed I at Bursa is a milestone in the history of Ottoman tilework. Inside are monochrome blue and green gilded tiles, *cuerda seca* tiles and tile mosaic of superb quality. The style of the tile mosaic is quite unlike that produced in Anatolia a century earlier, while the use of *cuerda seca* was unknown in Turkey at this time. As Julian Raby has pointed out, 'the aesthetic is Iranian and one can presume that Nakkaş 'Ali was inspired by the tiled splendours of contemporary Samarqand and Herat and played a role in its adoption'. That foreign and in particular Iranian tilemakers were unquestionably involved is confirmed by the Persian inscription on the tiles, *'amal-i ustadan-i Tabriz* (made by the masters of Tabriz).

For the next fifty years, these 'masters of Tabriz' continued to find work in Turkey. In 1425 they made the tiles in the mosque of Murad II in Bursa, after which they appear to have abandoned the technique of tile mosaic. They worked on a series of buildings in and around Edirne: the Şah Melek Paşa Camii in 1429 and the mosque of Murad II in 1436, where these remarkable craftsmen made a superb *cuerda seca mihrab* as well as the chinoiserie blue-and-white underglaze tiles referred to earlier (see page 95). A final commission in Edirne was the tilework in the Üç Şerefeli mosque between 1438 and 1448.

88 OPPOSITE
Rectangular tile, stone-paste, painted in underglaze black and blue. Egypt or Syria, first half of 15th century. The peacock is surrounded by foliage inspired by 14th-century Chinese blue-and-white.
HT: 26.15 cm.

89 Detail of one of four tiles over a metre high in situ on the Sunnet Odasi (Circumcision chamber) at Topkapi Saray. Probably Istanbul, first half of 16th century.

The Tabrizi craftsmen continued to work in Turkey until about the 1470s (their last work is in the tomb of Cem Sultan at Bursa (c.1474), expanding their range of colours until they were producing tiles which looked deceptively like *cuerda seca* but were actually painted under the glaze. Examples of these tiles are in the mosque of Mehmed II in Istanbul (built 1463–70). However, the 'masters of Tabriz' were not the only Iranian potters active in Turkey. Tile cutters from the east Iranian province of Khurasan may have worked on the Çinili Kösk, built within the grounds of the Topkapi Saray in 1472. Here, not only the use of glazed bricks (*banna'i*), unknown otherwise in Turkey, and tile mosaic, abandoned by the 'masters of Tabriz' after 1425, but the style of the building itself, with it stone-framed brick panels, is likely to have been inspired by some no longer extant Timurid or Turkman monument.

90 OPPOSITE Detail of *cuerda seca* tiles in situ on the façade of the throne room in Topkapi Saray. Probably Istanbul, first half of 16th century.

At the beginning of the sixteenth century references to Iranian tilemakers appear once again. In a royal wage register of 1526, published by Atasoy and Raby, is a reference to a certain Habib from Tabriz who was 'given his post because of his skill' and ten assistants recruited from all parts of the Ottoman empire. Like Timur, the Ottoman Sultan Selim (1512–20) also carried off

craftsmen and artists as prizes of war in addition to booty, and a number were taken following the defeat of the Safavids at the battle of Çaldiran in 1514. This Habib may have been among them. Between the 1520s and early 1550s, further tilework in *cuerda seca* can be seen on a number of monuments in Istanbul such as the façade of the throne room in the Topkapi Saray. The tilework of this period is distinctive for the tightness of the arabesque designs and the brilliant apple green and yellow of the colour scheme. 90

While *cuerda seca* continued to be the predominant technique used on tiles of the first half of the sixteenth century, a technical revolution was taking place at Iznik. Previously the centre of production of an earthenware often referred to as 'Miletus' ware, from about the 1470s the Iznik potters had begun making high-quality vessels from a pure white stone-paste, with bright clear colours under transparent glazes, arguably the finest Islamic pottery ever produced.

The focus of Iznik's production until the mid sixteenth century was on the manufacture of vessels. During this period, while only a very few tiles are thought to have been made at Iznik, the under-glaze technique began to be used by the school of tilemakers in Istanbul in addition to their work in *cuerda seca*. Gülru Necipoğlu has argued that the four spectacular panels over a metre high, 89 attributable to the 1520s, which in the seventeenth century were set into the walls of the circumcision chamber in the Topkapi Saray, were produced by the Istanbul workshop and not at Iznik. Made in one piece and painted in brilliant blue with turquoise on a white ground, they are exquisitely decorated with animals amid abundant foliage. The design of the leaves and overblown flowers 93 shows parallels with contemporary drawings of birds and serrated-edge *saz* leaves in the Topkapi Saray library and is likely to have been provided by the court atelier. John Carswell has recently argued that the animals at the base may have been influenced by drawings in a sketchbook in the Louvre by Jacobo Bellini, brother of Gentile Bellini, who was in Istanbul during the reign of Mehmed the Conqueror in the mid fifteenth century.

The location of the Istanbul workshop is not yet known for certain, but it has been convincingly argued that it is likely to have been within the confines of the Topkapi Saray or close by at the Tekfur Saray on the Golden Horn, site of the eighteenth-century revival ceramic factory. The Istanbul workshops producing both underglaze and *cuerda seca* executed only limited numbers of tiles and in about 1550 production was abruptly transferred to Iznik.

From the 1550s, the potteries found themselves fulfilling a demand for tiles fuelled by the building projects of Sultan Süleyman the Magnificent (1520–66). The first of these architectural projects was the refurbishment of the Dome of the Rock in Jerusalem. For this, one of the group of Tabriz tilemakers, ʿAbdallah Tabrizi, led a team of craftsmen who, on site, produced tiles in tile mosaic, *cuerda seca* and underglaze which have dates inscribed on them of AH 952/AD 1545 and 959/1551–2. In Damascus, Süleyman commissioned the Süleymaniye mosque and *madrasah* in 1554, whose tiles are likely to have been made by the same group of craftsmen once they had completed the Jerusalem commission. It is they who are credited with the establishment of the Damascus tile industry, discussed further below. In Istanbul, the Süleymaniye mosque complex, built by the Sultan's architect Sinan and inaugurated in 1557, set a trend for a whole series of magnificent tile commissions.

Coinciding with this increased interest in tilework in the mid sixteenth century were three developments. Firstly, the *cuerda seca* technique was finally abandoned; secondly, a new underglaze colour, a brilliant relief red known as 'Armenian bole' was introduced; and thirdly, a major stylistic change occurred in which a

(marginal figure references: 1–2, 113)

91 *Cuerda seca* tile, stone-paste, painted in blue, turquoise and black, from Jerusalem, part of the refurbishment of the Dome of the Rock in the mid 16th century. 18.5×18.5 cm

92 Three tiles, stone-paste, with the same design of a split-leaf palmette painted in *cuerda seca*, underglaze blue and black, with transparent and turquoise glaze. The first two come from the Dome of the Rock in Jerusalem and were part of the refurbishment of the mosque in the mid 16th century ordered by Süleyman the Magnificent. The third may have come from Syria. That the potters moved from Jerusalem to Syria is known from similar underglaze-painted tiles in Aleppo in houses such as Bayt Jumblat. Average dimensions: 18.5×18.5 cm.

new naturalistic range of flora was depicted. There is a well-defined chronology for Iznik thanks to the work of Arthur Lane, based on the existence of a number of dated pieces. Previous to the 93– phase of the mid 1550s are a number of types, including vessels painted in blue-and-white echoing Chinese porcelain and another of the 1530s to 1550s, painted in cobalt blue, turquoise, sage green, purple and grey with fantastic plant forms, known as the 'Damascus' group. Tiles belonging to these two groups are very rare. The earliest blue-and-white tiles still in situ are at the tomb of Şehzade Mahmud (1506–7) and in the tomb of Şehzade Ahmed (1512–13), both in Bursa, and at the mosque of Çoban Mustafa Paşa in Gebze (c.1529). 'Damascus' palette tiles are in the Yeni Kaplica baths in Bursa, restored by Süleyman the Magnificent's vizier, Rüstem Paşa (d. 1561), with an important group in the Ibrahim Paşa mosque in Istanbul, built in 1550.

The brilliant new red, an iron-rich slip thickly applied to 97– prevent it from running under the glaze, transformed the character of Iznik. An elegant floral style with realistic drawings of tulips, hyacinths, carnations and other flowers appears on both vessels and tiles and indeed on textiles, bookbindings and other arts of sixteenth-century Turkey. Other characteristic designs were the serrated edge *saz* leaf and, showing the still-present Chinese influence, large overblown lotus flowers, delicate prunus 101 blossoms and grape motifs.

It is interesting to note that while in the first phase of Ottoman tilework there was evidently a vogue for tiles in the Timurid taste, the Timurid obsession for covering entire façades in tiles never caught on. The Çinili Kösk, as noted earlier, is an exception, as is the Dome of the Rock. The fact that Ottoman architecture is largely stone and not brick was evidently the overriding factor. However, even when, after the mid sixteenth century, underglaze tiles began to be used more extensively, generally the exteriors of

93 Hexagonal tile, stone-paste, painted in underglaze blue and turquoise. Iznik, *c.*1540–50. The beautifully drawn ducks at the base of the tile are surrounded by serrated-edge *saz* leaves and overblown lotus flowers. 28.5×24.5 cm.

94 BELOW Rectangular tile, stone-paste, with underglaze-painted stencilled designs in blue and turquoise. Iznik, first half of 16th century. Chinese influence can be seen in the lotus flowers of the central cartouche which are combined with Islamic arabesques. 18.5×27.5 cm.

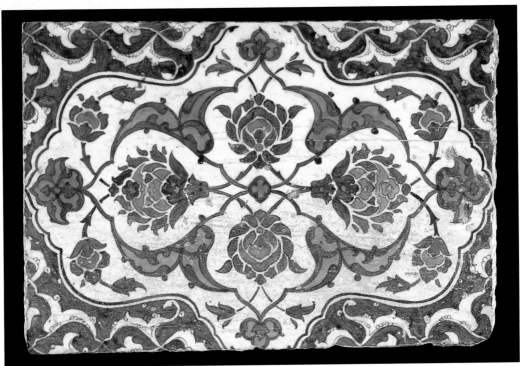

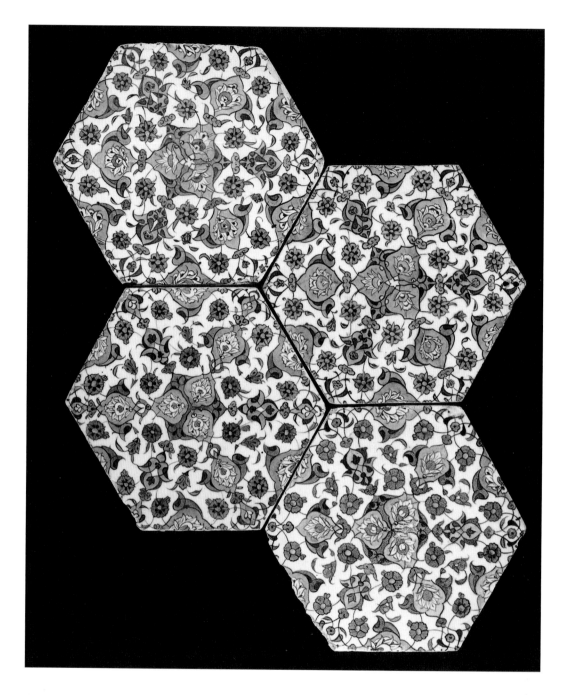

95 Hexagonal tiles with underglaze-painted
stencilled designs in blue and turquoise. Iznik,
first half of 16th century. The style is
associated with tiles on the façade of the
Circumcision chamber in Topkapi Saray.
Average DIAM: 21.5 cm.

96 Panel of three square tiles, stone-paste, painted in underglaze blue and turquoise with *saz* leaves and overgrown lotus flowers. Iznik, second half of 16th century. The use of blue-and-white colour scheme and the combination of chinoiserie flowers and *saz* leaves continued throughout the 16th century. These tiles are associated with the mosque of Eyyup on the Golden Horn. Each tile: 33×33 cm.

97 Four tiles, stone-paste, from a panel,
underglaze-painted in blue, emerald green and
red with large split-leaf palmettes and
overblown lotus blossoms on curling stems.
Iznik, second half of 16th century. Each tile:
21×21 cm.

Ottoman buildings were treated very differently. Tiles are found in limited areas, adding splashes of colour here and there to the sombre monumental architecture. Inside, tiles often emphasise particular areas such as the *mihrab*. One of the most splendid examples are panels surrounding the *mihrab* and elsewhere in Sokullu Mehmed Paşa Camii, built by Süleyman's architect Sinan (completed 1571). There are occasional examples of densely tiled interiors. The mosque of Rüstem Paşa (d. 1561), for instance, is covered from wall to wall in tiling, and there are a number of tombs such as that of Süleyman within the Süleymaniye complex where even the pendentives are covered in tiles; the Baghdad Kösk and Harem in Topkapi, with tiles of several different periods, are other examples. But this method of decoration was by no means the rule.

Standards at the Iznik potteries remained high for about a century. There was a huge demand – most buildings of the period had tiles somewhere, as apparently did the sultan's barge.

98 Four tiles, stone-paste, from a border panel, underglaze-painted in blue, emerald green and red. Iznik, second half of 16th century. The tulips, carnations and roses, lying on the white ground in the centre and reserved against the brilliant red ground on the borders, are typical of the best period of Iznik polychrome. 31×42.5 cm.

99 RIGHT Rectangular tile, stone-paste, from a border panel, underglaze-painted in blue, turquoise, emerald green and red. Iznik, second half of 16th century. 23.5×25.5 cm.

100 BELOW RIGHT Square tile, stone-paste, from a border panel, underglaze-painted in blue, emerald green and red. The flowers are outlined in dark blue and filled with a stippled blue ground. Iznik, second half of 16th century. 24×24 cm.

101 OPPOSITE Square tile, stone-paste, from a border panel, underglaze-painted in blue, emerald green and red. Iznik, second half of 16th century. The grape motif, inspired by Chinese porcelain, was popular with the Iznik potters. Here the clusters of grapes on a white ground are strikingly contrasted with the *saz* leaf and rosette reserved against the blue ground. 22×23 cm.

102 OVERLEAF, LEFT Underglaze-painted stone-paste tile with a stylised depiction of the Ka'ba at Mecca, mid 17th century. HT: 61 cm. The inscriptions in *naskhi* script give the names of the various gates and shrines within the sanctuary and, at the top, v. 96–7 from the Qur'an, *surah* 3, refer to the shrine and the importance of pilgrimage. Donative tiles such as these were produced in the mid 17th century and are among the last products of the Iznik potteries before decline set in.

02 However, although Iznik was still producing tiles and vessels during the seventeenth century, standards were beginning to drop and edicts from the court complain not only of poor-quality tiles but that they were sometimes not delivered on time. The potters were diversifying into markets other than the court, and commissions for tile revetments came from as far away as Egypt, Hungary, Moldavia and Mount Athos. By the end of the seventeenth century, however, the Iznik factories were producing little and a group of potters were transferred from Iznik to Istanbul, where they set up the Tekfur Saray factory near Eyyup on the Golden Horn producing revivalist Iznik tiles.

KÜTAHYA

After the demise of the Iznik workshops in the seventeenth century, pottery continued to be produced in Turkey at Kütahya, a town on the edge of the Anatolian plateau about 200 km southeast of Istanbul. Known in fact to have had kilns since at least the beginning of the sixteenth century echoing, at least in this early period, the wares of Iznik, it is not clear what they were making

103 OVERLEAF, RIGHT Rectangular tile, stone-paste, painted in underglaze polychrome colours including blue, turquoise and yellow, depicting an Old Testament scene and with an Armenian inscription below. Kütahya, 18th–19th century. 26×19 cm.

104 ABOVE Rectangular tile, stone-paste, underglaze-painted in green, yellow and brown with angels and crosses. Kütahya, 18th century. Similar designs are found on ceramic eggs placed above oil lamps still found in the Armenian Cathedral in Jerusalem. 11.5×23.5 cm.

105 RIGHT Fragmentary tile, stone-paste, painted in underglaze blue, yellow and black with a figure, probably a saint, holding a cross. Kütahya, 18th–19th century. 9.5×10 cm.

106 OPPOSITE Icon of the Virgin and Child, made up of two tiles, stone-paste, painted in underglaze blue, yellow, black and red. Kütahya, 18th–19th century. 10.5×13.7 cm.

107 Square tile, stone-paste. Syria, 16th century. Reserved in white against the blue ground are a fantastic tree, overblown rosettes and *saz* leaves, in designs and underglaze colours very similar to Iznik plates produced between 1540 and 1560. 26.8×26.8 cm.

after that, and only from the eighteenth century can we be reasonably certain of the type of pottery they produced.

Small bowls, plates and jugs, either in blue-and-white or in a colourful palette which included yellow and green, show the influence of Japanese Kakiemon porcelain. The vessels are generally decorated with either floral designs or quaint figures in wide kaftans and balloon trousers. Tiles were also produced, including icons of the Virgin and Child or with designs of winged angels; the most important series are in the Armenian Cathedral of St James in Jerusalem (1718–19). In the nineteenth century the Kütahya kilns were producing Iznik revival wares, and after the First World War a group of Kütahya potters settled in Jerusalem to work on the restoration of the Dome of the Rock tiles. Both the Kütahya and the Jerusalem potteries are still active today.

THE OTTOMAN PROVINCES

In the Ottoman provinces, polychrome tiles strongly influenced by Iznik were produced at Diyarbakir in Anatolia. The Damascus potteries, which had produced the blue-and-white tiles in the early

108 Three underglaze tiles, stone-paste, from a panel painted in delicate underglaze blue, turquoise and sage green. The narrow border, which is incorporated into the tile, has a scrolling design of rosettes and lotus blossoms against a blue ground. This contrasts with the central motif of flowers entwined around wavy bands on a white ground. Syria, 16th century. Average dimensions: 29×37 cm.

109 OVERLEAF, ABOVE LEFT Hexagonal tile, stone-paste, underglaze-painted in black under a turquoise glaze. Syria, second half of 16th century. The design of clusters of dots and tiger stripes has possible Central Asian derivation and was a popular motif in Ottoman art, particularly in ceramics and textiles. DIAM: 29.5 cm.

110 OVERLEAF, ABOVE RIGHT Rectangular tile, stone-paste, painted in delicate underglaze blues, green and manganese, with a peacock surrounded by scrolls of hyacinths and other flowers springing from a central point. Syria, 17th century. 24×28 cm.

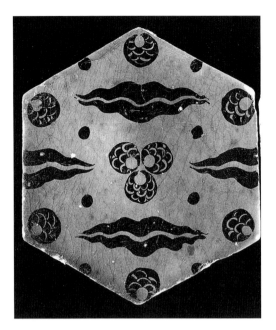

113 Detail of underglaze tiles in situ in the Süleymaniye mosque in Damascus, 16th century.

113

7–12

fifteenth century, were given fresh stimulus a century later. The building of the Damascus Süleymaniye and the city's enhanced status as an important Ottoman provincial capital gave rise to a series of buildings throughout Syria – mosques, tombs and grand houses – decorated with tilework. The hand of the Jerusalem potters who restored the Dome of the Rock is evident in tiles, particularly in Aleppo.

The Syrian tile designs echo those of Iznik but are painted with an exuberance and spirit far removed from their more formal Iznik counterparts where the designs were evidently more strictly controlled by the court. The magnificent floral schemes of the sixteenth and seventeenth century are seen in a number of mosques such as the Darwishiyah in Damascus. And, brought back to England by Lord Leighton, there are magnificent Syrian tile panels in the Arab Hall of his house in Holland Park and other fine panels in the Victoria and Albert Museum. Syrian tiles are painted under the glaze in characteristic soft greens, turquoise and aubergine, the colours used by the Iznik potters of the 1540s. (It was the use of these colours in Syria that give rise to the confusing description of that particular phase of Iznik as the 'Damascus' group.) Favourite designs were large-scale floral repeat patterns and the frequent presence on the panels of vases brimful of flowers; the realistic shapes of tankards and bottles are copied from both Iznik and Syrian pottery. The best period for the Damascus potteries was the sixteenth century after which, although tiles continued to be produced until the nineteenth century, the quality progressively diminishes and standardisation sets in.

111 OPPOSITE, BELOW LEFT Rectangular underglaze-painted border tile, stone-paste. Syria, 16th–17th century. Against a blue ground are *saz* leaves painted in turquoise filled with chinoiserie cloud bands, split-leaf palmettes and rosettes reserved in white and painted in green and manganese with black outlines. 28.5×15 cm.

112 OPPOSITE, BELOW RIGHT Two rectangular tiles, stone-paste, from a group of nine forming part of a lunette panel in sage green, manganese, turquoise and blue. Syria, 16th–17th century. The colours are typical of Damascus tiles of this period and the delicately drawn tulips and carnations echo the designs on the metropolitan Ottoman production of Iznik. Average dimensions each tile: 30.5 cm.

114 Detail from a panel of De Morgan tiles designed by Halsey Ricardo in the entrance of 8 Addison Road, London, built for Sir Ernest Debenham in 1904. The design and colour scheme are inspired by Ottoman pottery. This was one of the final commissions of the De Morgan factory before its closure in 1911.

THE INFLUENCE ON EUROPE

Islamic pottery and tilework were hugely influential on the ceramics of Europe. The introduction of the tin glaze into Islamic Spain was the first step in the great tradition of Hispano-Moresque pottery seen in the magnificent wares of Manises, Granada, Valencia and other centres. In succeeding centuries, the tin glaze technique was adopted in other parts of Europe; Italian maiolica and Delft ware were ultimately the result of this spread of techniques originating in the Islamic lands.

In the nineteenth century Europe experienced a renewed fascination with Islamic pottery. The vogue for travel to the biblical lands of the Levant introduced the West to the pottery and tilework of Turkey and the Ottoman provinces. Tiles, which had become collectable, were stripped from dilapidated houses and mosques in Syria and Palestine for sale in Europe. Persian lustre tiles, too, came into fashion. The tiles from both these regions had one particular feature in common for Western collectors: not only could they be appreciated in their original form as complete panels, but also as single decorative objects. This regional bias is reflected in the strengths of the British Museum's and other collections formed at this time. In contrast, Central Asia and Afghanistan during the latter part of the nineteenth century were areas where Western powers were playing out the 'Great Game'. They were therefore more difficult to reach and only intrepid adventurers and army officers dared go there. In any case, the characteristic tilework of this region, tile mosaic and *cuerda seca*, did not have the same visual appeal in the West.

Ottoman tiles particularly appealed to the imagination of nineteenth-century artists. The Orientalist painter Jean-Léon Gérôme (1824–1904) featured a panel of carefully rendered seventeenth-century Iznik tiles in *The Moorish Bath*. Such was the interest in Ottoman wares in ceramic factories in England and France that a number of potters began to copy both the designs and the glazes of Iznik and Damascus wares. Theodore Deck (1823–91), who worked for the Sèvres pottery, analysed the Iznik glaze and created Iznik style vessels during the 1860s. Colin Minton, head of the Minton factory, is known to have purchased Iznik tiles in Paris and Istanbul in order to study and imitate the colours and glazes. Although they had great difficulty reproducing the Iznik red (the Islamic potters also found red difficult to achieve), Minton made passable imitations of Iznik tiles. At the Paris exhibition of 1867, tiles in the Ottoman style were shown by both French and English ceramic factories. It is William De Morgan (1839–1917), however, who was arguably the most adept and inspired of the Orientalist potters. Not only did he reinvent Islamic lustre, but his complete mastery of the colours and glazes of Ottoman pottery – the 'Persian' style, as he called it (everything Islamic tended to be called Persian at that time) – led to the important commission in 1879 to work on Leighton House. Lord Leighton's superb tile collection was being set into the Arab Hall and De Morgan not only created a beautiful background of turquoise tiles for them, but, where the originals had been broken, he made extremely good imitations to replace them.

In the twentieth century the variety of tiles produced in the countries of the Islamic world is extremely diverse. In countries such as Morocco, where the art of tilework (*zillij*) is very much alive, tilemakers are continuing to evolve and to innovate within a distinctive tradition. Turkey provides a contrasting example, manufacturing high-quality mass-produced copies of Iznik tiles destined for foreign as much as domestic markets. Meanwhile a number of artists in the Middle East have begun to find expression in the creation of ceramic tiles. At the present time, therefore, the diversity of tiles in the Islamic world is greater than ever before. However, it is a diversity now shaped as much by outside influences as by indigenous tradition.

114

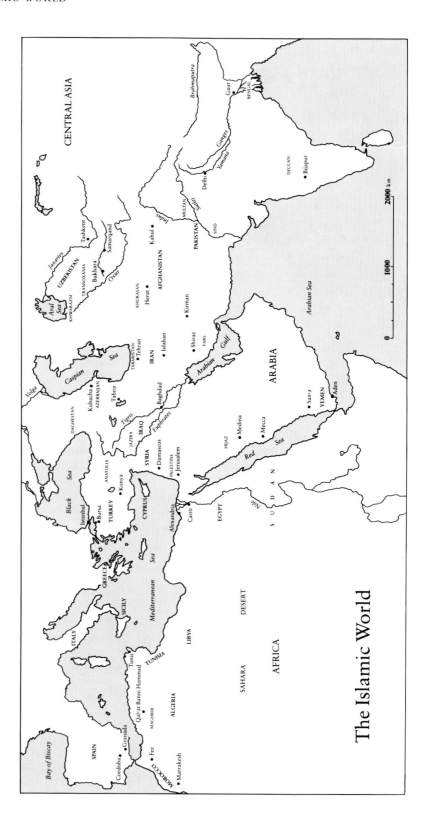

The Islamic World

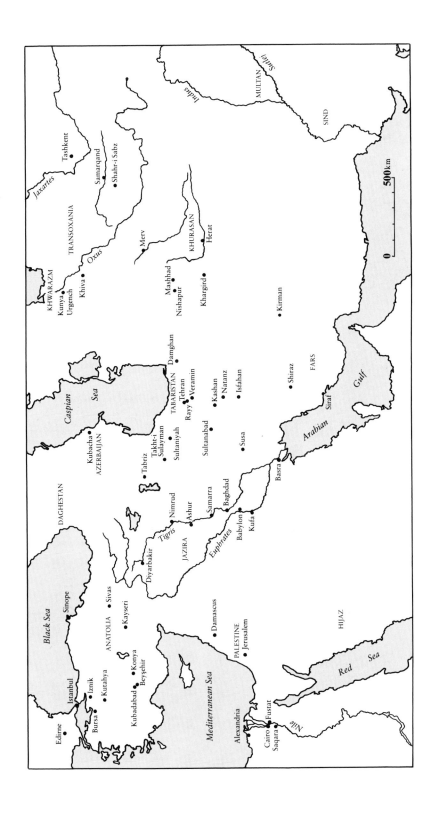

FURTHER READING

This selected bibliography is not intended to be comprehensive but a guide to further reading and to provide references for works cited in the text.

GENERAL WORKS

Ali, Abdullah Yusuf (trans.). *The meaning of the Glorious Qur'an*, London, 1975

The Arts of Islam, Hayward Gallery (exh. cat.), London, 1976

Blair, S. and J. Bloom, *The Art and Architecture of Islam 1250–1800*, New Haven and London, 1995

Brend, B. *Islamic Art*, London, 1991

Bosworth, C.E. *The Islamic Dynasties*, 1980

Ettinghausen, R. and O. Grabar. *The Art and Architecture of Islam 650–1250*, Harmondsworth, 1987

Lane, A. *Early Islamic Pottery*, London, 1947

Lane, A. *Later Islamic Pottery*, London, 1957

Rogers, J.M. *Islamic Art and Design 1500–1700*, London, 1983

Wilson, E. *Islamic Designs*, London, 1991

GENERAL WORKS ON TILES

Carboni, S. and T. Masuya. *Persian Tiles*, Metropolitan Museum of Art, New York, 1993

Lane, A. *A Guide to the Collection of Tiles*, London, 1960

Öney, G. *Ceramic tiles in Islamic Architecture*, Istanbul, 1987

Scarce, J.M. 'Tilework' in Ferrier (ed.), *The Arts of Persia*, New Haven and London, 1989

CHAPTER 1

Allan, J.W. 'Abu'l-Qasim's treatise on Ceramics', *Iran* XI, 1973, pp. 111–20

Caiger-Smith, A. *Lustre Pottery*, London, 1985

Caiger-Smith, A. *Tin Glaze Pottery*, London, 1973

Centlivres-Demont, M. *Une communauté de potiers en Iran*, Wiesbaden, 1971

Hedgecoe, J. and S.S. Damluji. *Zillij: The Art of Moroccan Ceramics*, Reading, 1992

Wulff, H.E. *The Traditional Crafts of Persia*, Cambridge, Mass., 1966

CHAPTER 2

Bahgat, A. and F. Massoul, *La céramique Musulmane de l'Egypte*, Cairo, 1930

Creswell, K.A.C., in J.W. Allan (ed.). *A short account of Early Muslim Architecture*, Oxford, 1989

Dayton, J. *Minerals, Metals, Glazing and Man*, London, 1978

Golvin, L. *Recherches archaeologiques à la Qala des Banu Hamad*, Paris, 1965

Kraeling, C.H. *The Excavations at Dura Europos: Final Report*, VIII, part I, *The Synagogue*, New Haven, 1956

Kühnel, E. 'Die 'Abbasidischen Lüsterfayencen', *Ars Islamica* I, 1934, pp. 149–59

Marçais, G. *Les faiences à reflêts métalliques de la Grande Mosquée de Kairouan*, Paris, 1928

Mason, R. and E.J. Keall. 'The 'Abbasid glazed wares of Siraf and the Basra connection: Petrographic analysis', *Iran* XXIX, 1991, pp. 51–68

Moorey, P.R.S. *Materials and Manufacture in Ancient Mesopotamia*, BAR International Series 237, Oxford, 1985

Sarre, F. *Die keramik von Samarra*, Berlin, 1925

Stevenson-Smith, W. *The Art and Architecture of Ancient Egypt*, London, 1990

CHAPTER 3

Guchani, A. *Persian poetry on the tiles of Takht-i Sulayman* (in Farsi), Tehran, n.d.

Kiani, M.Y., F. Karimi and A. Guchani. *Introduction to the art of Iranian tile work in the Islamic period*, Tehran, 1983

Meinecke, M. *Fayencedekorationen seldschhkischer Sakralbauten in Kleinasien*, Tübingen, 1976

Melikian-Chirvani, A.S. 'Le Livre des Rois, Mirroir du Destin. II–Takht-e Soleyman et la Symbolique du Shah-name', *Studia Iranica* 20, 1991, pp. 33–148

Naumann, R. 'Brennöfen für Glasurkeramik', *Istanbuler Mitteilungen* 21, 1977, pp. 173–90

Naumann, R. *Takht-i Suleiman* (exh. cat.), Prähistorischen Staatssammlung, Munich, 1976

Öney, G. 'Kubadabad Ceramics', in *The Art of Iran and Anatolia*, Percival David Foundation Colloquies on Art and Archaeology in Asia, no. 4, London, 1974, pp. 68–85

Scerrato, U. 'Islamic glazed tiles with moulded decoration from Ghazni', *East and West*, n.s. vol. 13, no. 4, 1962, pp. 263–87

Shreve-Simpson, M. 'The Narrative structure of a medieval Iranian beaker', *Ars Orientalis* 12, 1981, pp. 15–22

Watson, O. *Persian Lustre Ware*, London, 1985

Wilkinson, C.K. *Nishapur: Some early Islamic buildings and their decoration*, New York, 1987

CHAPTER 4

Carswell, J. *New Julfa Armenian churches and other buildings*, Oxford, 1968

Clavijo, R.G. de, G. Le Strange (trans.). *Clavijo Embassy to Tamerlane 1403–1406*, New York, 1928

Gobineau, le Comte de. *Trois ans en Asie*, Paris, 1923

Golombek, L. and D. Wilber. *Timurid Architecture of Iran and Turan*, 2 vols, Princeton, 1988

Guy, J. and D. Swallow (eds). *Arts of India 1550–1900*, London, 1990

Hillenbrand, R. 'The use of glazed tilework in Iranian Islamic architecture', *Akten des VII Internationalen Kongresses für Islamische Kunst und Archäologie*, Munich, 1976, pp. 545–54

Lentz, T.W. and G.D. Lowry, *Timur and the Princely Vision*, Los Angeles, 1989

Lerner, J.D. 'Three Achaemenid "Fakes"', *Expedition* 22, 1980, pp. 5–16

Luschey-Schmeisser, I. *The pictorial cycle of Hasht Behesht*

in Isfahan and its iconographic tradition, Rome, 1978

Nath, R. *Colour decoration in Mughal architecture*, Bombay, 1970

O'Kane, B. *Timurid Architecture in Khurasan*, Mazda Press, 1977

Pietro della Valle. *The journey of Pietro della Valle the pilgrim*, London, 1989

Scarce, J.M. 'Function and Decoration in Qajar Tilework', in *Persian art and culture of the 18th and 19th centuries*, Edinburgh, 1979

Scarce, J.M. 'Ali Mohammed Isfahani, Tilemaker of Tehran', *Oriental Art*, n.s. 22, 1976

Tavernier, J.B. *The six Voyages of John Baptiste Tavernier*, London, 1678

Wilber, D. 'The development of mosaic faience in Islamic architecture in Iran', *Ars Islamica* VI, 1939, pp. 16–47

CHAPTER 5

Atasoy, N. and J. Raby, *Iznik: The pottery of Ottoman Turkey*, London, 1989

Atil, E. *Renaissance of Islam: Art of the Mamluks*, Washington, DC, 1981

Beveridge, A.S. *The Babur-nama in English*, London, 1969

Carswell, J. 'Ceramics', in Y. Petsopoulos (ed.), *Tulips, Arabesques and Turbans: Decorative arts from the Ottoman empire*, London, 1982, pp. 73–121

Carswell, J. 'Some fifteenth-century hexagonal tiles from the Near-east', *Victoria and Albert Museum Yearbook* III, 1972, pp. 59–75

Carswell, J. and C.J.F. Dowsett. *Kütahya Tiles and Pottery from the Armenian Cathedral of St James, Jerusalem*, 2 vols, London, 1972

Carswell, J. '"The feast of the Gods": The porcelain trade between China, Istanbul and

Venice', *Asian Affairs* XXIV, II, June 1993, pp. 180–6

Catleugh, J. *William de Morgan Tiles*, New York, 1983

Goodwin, G. *A History of Ottoman Architecture*, London, 1992

Meinecke, M. 'Syrian Blue-and-white Tiles of the 9th/15th Century', *Damaszener Mitteilungen* 3, 1988, pp. 203–14

Necipoğlu, G. 'From International Timurid to Ottoman: A change of taste in sixteenth-century ceramic tiles', *Muqarnas* VII, 1990, pp. 136–70

Raby, J. 'Diyarbakir: A rival to Iznik: a sixteenth-century tile industry in Eastern Anatolia', *Istanbuler Mitteilungen* Bd. 27/8, 1977–8

Rogers, J.M. and R.M. Ward, *Süleyman the Magnificent* (exh. cat.), London, 1988

ILLUSTRATION
ACKNOWLEDGEMENTS

Accession numbers of objects in the British Museum are prefixed by Department: OA *(Oriental Antiquities)* or WA *(Western Asiatic).*

Frontispiece OA G.1983.499, Godman Bequest
1 Photo by St John Simpson
2 Drawn by Ann Searight, after Naumann, 1977, fig. 95
3 OA G.1983.206, Godman Bequest
4 OA G.1983.476, Godman Bequest
5 OA G.1983.495, Godman Bequest
6 Photo by author
7 Photo by author
8 Drawn by Eva Wilson, 1991, no. 5, after Art Institute of Chicago (1926.1186), Logan-Pattern-Ryerson Collection
9 WA 90859
10 OA+2271, +10624.1 & 2, +10625
11 OA+2277, +10842(9) & (12)
12 Courtesy Museum für Islamische Kunst, Berlin (Sam 785a)
13 Drawn by Ann Searight, after Sarre, 1925, fig. 121
14 Drawn by Ann Searight, after Marçais, 1928, figs 25, 38, 88, 16
15 Drawn by Ann Searight, after Bahgat & Massoul, 1930, pl. 130
16 Courtesy Musée des Arts Décoratifs, Paris (on loan to the Institut du Monde Arabe 14869)
17 OA G.1983.211, 212, 219 & 229, Godman Bequest
18 OA G.1983.204, Godman Bequest
19 OA G.1983.451-454, 478, 480, 483, Godman Bequest, OA 1896.2-1.101
20 OA G.1983.205, Godman Bequest
21 OA G.1983.230, 231 & 232A & B, Godman Bequest
22 OA 1878.12-30.573(2), Henderson Bequest
23 OA 1954.12-15.1, given by Alfred Speers
24 OA 1923.10-19.1
25 OA+10792, 10796, 10795, 10801(2), 10799 & 10800
26 OA G.1983.500, Godman Bequest
27 OA 1878.12-30.568, 569 & 570, Henderson Bequest
28 OA G.1983.190, Godman Bequest
29 OA 1896.3-14.32
30 OA G.1983.221, 222, 223 & 224, Godman Bequest
31 OA 1888.1-9.3
32 OA G.1983.487, Godman Bequest
33 Courtesy Museum of Fine Arts, Boston, Ross collection (07.903)
34 OA 1878.12-30.561, Henderson Bequest

35 OA+1123
36 OA+1123 (back)
37 Courtesy Keir collection, Ham, Richmond (73.5.42)
38 Courtesy Freer Gallery of Art, Smithsonian Institution, Washington, DC (43.3)
39 OA G.1983.487, Godman Bequest
40 Courtesy Metropolitan Museum of Art, New York, Edward C. Moore collection, Bequest of Edward C. Moore, 1891 (91.1.105)
41 Courtesy Metropolitan Museum of Art, New York, purchase Joseph Pulitzer Bequest (52.20.1)
42 Drawn by Eva Wilson, 1991, no. 13, after Victoria and Albert Museum (C444-1911)
43 Photo courtesy Oliver Watson
44 OA+1122
45 OA G.1983.194, Godman Bequest
46 OA G.1983.196, Godman Bequest
47 OA+10828
48 OA G.1983.499, Godman Bequest
49 & 50 OA G.1983.493 & 1907.6-10.2, given by Sir Thomas D. Gibson Carmichael through National Art Collections Fund
51 OA 1894.5-11.1
52 OA G.1983.484, Godman Bequest
53 Courtesy Metropolitan Museum of Art, New York, Gift of Marjorie Shwarz in memory of Herbert F. and Dorothy C. Schwarz, 1975 (1975.193.4)
54 Courtesy Metropolitan Museum of Art, New York, Rogers Fund, 1937 (37.40.24)
55 Courtesy Board of Trustees of the Victoria and Albert Museum, London (344-1906)
56 Photo by Margaret Oliphant
57 With permission of Dr Qassem Toueir
58 OA 1948.12-11.07
59 OA 1908.8-4.9 & 11
60 Photo by author
61 Photo by author
62 OA 1907.10-11.1
63 OA G.1983.486, Godman Bequest
64 OA 1908.8-4.1, 2 & 3
65 OA 1952.7-22.1, given by the Director of the Victoria and Albert Museum
66 OA 1887.6-17.4
67 Photo by author
68 OA G.1983.501, Godman Bequest
69 Photo by author
70 Photo by author
71 OA collection
72 OA 1937.12-17.1

73 OA 1949.11-15.8, given by Mrs Percy Newberry
74 OA+10639
75 OA 1895.6-3.1, 2 & 3
76 OA 1891.5-18.1, given by E.A. Budge
77 OA 1981.6-4.3, Woodward Bequest
78 OA 1981.6-4.2
79 OA G.1983.314, Godman Bequest
80 OA 1951.10-8.3
81 OA+14438
82 OA 1895.6-3.152 & 154
83 OA 1856.12-16.1
84 OA 1993.10-27.1 & 2
85 OA 1978.4-19.1
86 OA 1954.12-15.2, given by Alfred Speers
87 OA 1895.6-3.138, Franks Bequest
88 OA 1905.11-28.1, given by Sydney Nacher
89 Photo by author
90 Photo by author
91 OA 1969.1-14.2
92 OA 1969.1-14.3 & 4, 1895.6-3.139, Franks Bequest
93 OA 1892.6-13.69, Franks Bequest
94 OA 1895.6-3.145, Franks Bequest
95 OA+623, 624, G.1983.12, Godman Bequest, 1887.6-17.23
96 OA 1878.12-30.534, Henderson Bequest
97 OA G.1983.77, Godman Bequest
98 OA G.1983.71, Godman Bequest
99 OA G.1983.117, Godman Bequest
100 OA 1887.6-17.31
101 OA G.1983.78, Godman Bequest
102 Courtesy Board of Trustees of the Victoria and Albert Museum, London (427-1900)
103 OA 1932.6-15.2
104 OA 1885.6-9.2
105 OA+10638
106 OA 1928.10-17.1
107 OA 1895.6-3.129, Franks Bequest
108 OA G.1983.98, Godman Bequest
109 OA 1887.6-17.28, given by Sir A.W. Franks
110 OA 1878.12-30.542, Henderson Bequest
111 OA 1895.6-3.135, Franks Bequest
112 OA 1922.4-11.1 & 2, given by Mrs Doughty
113 Photo by author
114 Photo by author

INDEX

Numbers in **bold** refer to figure numbers and captions.